Undergraduate Topics in Computer Sci

Undergraduate Topics in Computer Science (UTiCS) delivers high-quality instructional content for undergraduates studying in all areas of computing and information science. From core foundational and theoretical material to final-year topics and applications, UTiCS books take a fresh, concise, and modern approach and are ideal for self-study or for a one- or two-semester course. The texts are all authored by established experts in their fields, reviewed by an international advisory board, and contain numerous examples and problems. Many include fully worked solutions.

Also in this series

Iain D. Craig
Object-Oriented Programming Languages: Interpretation
978-1-84628-773-2

Max Bramer
Principles of Data Mining
978-1-84628-765-7

Hanne Riis Nielson and Flemming Nielson
Semantics with Applications: An Appetizer
978-1-84628-691-9

Michael Kifer and Scott A. Smolka
Introduction to Operating System Design and Implementation: The OSP 2 Approcah
978-1-84628-842-5

Phil Brooke and Richard Paige
Practical Distributed Processing
978-1-84628-840-1

Frank Klawonn
Computer Graphics with Java
978-1-84628-847-0

David Salomon
A Concise Introduction to Data Compression
978-1-84800-071-1

David Makinson
Sets, Logic and Maths for Computing
978-1-84628-844-9

Orit Hazzan
Agile Software Engineering
978-1-84800-198-5

Pankaj Jalote
A Concise Introduction to Software Engineering
978-1-84800-301-9

Alan P. Parkes
A Concise Introduction to Languages and Machines
978-1-84800-120-6

Gilles Dowek

Principles
of Programming
Languages

 Springer

Gilles Dowek
École Polytechnique
France

Undergraduate Topics in Computer Science ISSN 1863-7310
ISBN: 978-1-84882-031-9   e-ISBN: 978-1-84882-032-6
DOI: 10.1007/978-1-84882-032-6

British Library Cataloguing in Publication Data
A catalogue record for this book is available from the British Library

Library of Congress Control Number: 2008943965

Based on course notes by Gilles Dowek published in 2006 by L'Ecole Polytechnique with the following
title: "Les principes des langages de programmation."

Printed on acid-free paper

Springer Science+Business Media
springer.com

The author wants to thank François Pottier, Philippe Baptiste, Julien Cervelle, Albert Cohen, Olivier Delande, Olivier Hermant, Ian Mackie, François Morain, Jean-Marc Steyaert and Paul Zimmermann for their remarks on a first version of this book.

Preface

We've known about algorithms for millennia, but we've only been writing computer programs for a few decades. A big difference between the Euclidean or Eratosthenes age and ours is that since the middle of the twentieth century, we express the algorithms we conceive using formal languages: programming languages.

Computer scientists are not the only ones who use formal languages. Optometrists, for example, prescribe eyeglasses using very technical expressions, such as "OD: -1.25 (-0.50) 180° OS: -1.00 (-0.25) 180°", in which the parentheses are essential. Many such formal languages have been created throughout history: musical notation, algebraic notation, etc. In particular, such languages have long been used to control machines, such as looms and cathedral chimes.

However, until the appearance of programming languages, those languages were only of limited importance: they were restricted to specialised fields with only a few specialists and written texts of those languages remained relatively scarce. This situation has changed with the appearance of programming languages, which have a wider range of applications than the prescription of eyeglasses or the control of a loom, are used by large communities, and have allowed the creation of programs of many hundreds of thousands of lines.

The appearance of programming languages has allowed the creation of artificial objects, programs, of a complexity incomparable to anything that has come before, such as steam engines or radios. These programs have, in return, allowed the creation of other complex objects, such as integrated circuits made of millions of transistors, or mathematical proofs that are hundreds of thousands of pages long. It is very surprising that we have succeeded in writing such complex programs in languages comprising such a small number of constructs — assignment, loops, etc. — that is to say in languages barely more sophisticated than the language of prescription eyeglasses.

Programs written in these programming languages have the novelty of not only being understandable by humans, which brings them closer to the scores used by organists, but also readable by machines, which brings them closer to the punch cards used in Barbarie organs.

The appearance of programming languages has therefore profoundly impacted our relationship with language, complexity, and machines.

This book is an introduction to the principles of programming languages. It uses the Java language for support. It is intended for students who already have some experience with computer programming. It is assumed that they have learned some programming empirically, in a single programming language, other than Java.

The first objective of this book will then be to learn the fundamentals of the Java programming language. However, knowing a single programming language is not sufficient to be a good programmer. For this, you must not only know several languages, but be able to easily learn new ones. This requires that you understand universal concepts like functions or cells, which exist in one form or another in all programming languages. This can only be done by comparing two or more languages. In this book, two comparison languages have been chosen: Caml and C. Therefore, the goal is not for the students to learn three programming languages simultaneously, but that with the comparison with Caml and C, they can learn the principles around which programming languages are created. This understanding will allow them to develop, if they wish, a real competence in Caml or in C, or in any other programming language.

Another objective of this book is for the students to begin acquiring the tools which permit them to precisely define the meaning of the program. This precision is, indeed, the only means to clearly understand what happens when a program is executed, and to reason in situations where complexity defies intuition. The idea is to describe the meaning of a statement by a function operating on a set of states. However, our expectations of this objective remain modest: students wishing to pursue this goal will have to do so elsewhere.

The final objective of this course is to learn basic algorithms for lists and trees. Here too, our expectations remain modest: students wishing to pursue this will also have to look elsewhere.

Contents

1

Imperative Core

1.1 Five Constructs

Most programming languages have, among others, five constructs: assignment, variable declaration, sequence, test, and loop. These constructs form the *imperative core* of the language.

1.1.1 Assignment

The *assignment* construct allows the creation of a statement with a variable x and an expression t. In Java, this statement is written as x = t;. *Variables* are identifiers which are written as one of more letters. *Expressions* are composed of variables and constants with operators, such as +, -, *, / — division — and % — modulo.

Therefore, the following statements

```
x = y % 3;

x = y;

y = 3;

x = x + 1;
```

G. Dowek, *Principles of Programming Languages*,
Undergraduate Topics in Computer Science, DOI 10.1007/978-1-84882-032-6_1,
© Springer-Verlag London Limited 2009

are all proper Java statements, while

```
y + 3 = x;
```

```
x + 2 = y + 5;
```

are not.

To understand what happens when you execute the statement `x = t;` suppose that within the recesses of your computer's memory, there is a compartment labelled `x`. Executing the statement `x = t;` consists of filling this compartment with the *value* of the expression `t`. The value previously contained in compartment `x` is erased. If the expression `t` is a constant, for example 3, its value is the same constant. If it is an expression with no variables, such as 3 + 4, its value is obtained by carrying out mathematical operations, in this case, addition. If expression `t` contains variables, the values of these variables must be looked up in the computer's memory. The whole of the contents of the computer's memory is called a *state*.

Let us consider, initially, that expressions, such as `x + 3`, and statements, such as `y = x + 3;`, form two disjoint categories. Later, however, we shall be brought to revise this premise.

In these examples, the values of expressions are integers. Computers can only store integers within a finite interval. In Java, integers must be between -2^{31} and $2^{31} - 1$, so there are 2^{32} possible values. When a mathematical operation produces a value outside of this interval, the result is kept within the interval by taking its modulo 2^{32} remainder. Thus, by adding 1 to $2^{31} - 1$, that is to say 2147483647, we leave the interval and then return to it by removing 2^{32}, which gives -2^{31} or -2147483648.

Exercise 1.1

What is the value of the variable `x` after executing the following statement?

```
x = 2 * 1500000000;
```

In Caml, assignment is written `x := t`. *In the expression* `t`, *we designate the value of* `x`, *not with the expression* `x` *itself, but with the expression* `!x`. *Thus, in Caml we write* `y := !x + 1` *while in Java we write* `y = x + 1;`.

In C, assignment is written as it is in Java.

1.1.2 Variable Declaration

Before being able to assign values to a variable x, it must be declared, which associates the name x to a location in the computer's memory.

Variable declaration is a construct that allows the creation of a statement composed of a variable, an expression, and a statement. In Java, this statement is written {int x = t; p} where p is a statement, for example {int x = 4; x = x + 1;}. The variable x can then be used in the statement p, which is called the *scope* of variable x.

It is also possible to declare a variable without giving it an initial value, for example, {int x; x = y + 4;}. We must of course be careful not to use a variable which has been declared without an initial value and that has not been assigned a value. This produces an error.

Apart from the int type, Java has three other integer types that have different intervals. These types are defined in Table 1.1. When a mathematical operation produces a value outside of these intervals, the result is returned to the interval by taking its remainder, modulo the size of the interval.

In Java, there are also other *scalar types* for decimal numbers, booleans, and characters. These types are defined in Table 1.1. Operations allowed in the construction of expressions for each of these types are described in Table 1.2.

Variables can also contain objects that are of *composite types*, like arrays and character strings, which we will address later. Because we will need them shortly, character strings are described briefly in Table 1.3.

The integers are of type byte, short, int or long corresponding to the intervals $[-2^7, 2^7 - 1]$, $[-2^{15}, 2^{15} - 1]$, $[-2^{31}, 2^{31} - 1]$ and $[-2^{63}, 2^{63} - 1]$, Respectively. Constants are written in base 10, for example, -666.

Decimal numbers are of type float or double. Constants are written in scientific notation, for example 3.14159, 666 or 6.02E23.

Booleans are of type boolean. Constants are written as false and true.

Characters are of type char. Constants are written between apostrophes, for example 'b'.

Table 1.1 Scalars types in Java

To declare a variable of type T, replace the type int with T. The general form of a declaration is thus {T x = t; p}.

The basic operations that allow for arithmetical expressions are +, -, *, / — division — and % — modulo.

When one of the numbers a or b is negative, the number a / b is the quotient rounded towards 0. So the result of a / b is the quotient of the absolute values of a and b, and is positive when a and b have the same sign, and negative if they have different signs. The number a % b is a - b * (a / b). So (-29) / 4 equals -7 and (-29) % 4 equals -1.

The operations for decimal numbers are +, -, *, /, along with some transcendental functions: `Math.sin`, `Math.cos`, ...

The operations allowed in boolean expressions are ==, != — different —, <, >, <=, >=, & — and —, &&, | — or —, || and ! — not.

For all data types, the expression (b) ? t : u evaluates to the value of t if the boolean expression b has the value `true`, and evaluates to the value of u if the boolean expression b has the value `false`.

Table 1.2 Expressions in Java

Character strings are of type `String`. Constants are written inside quotation marks, for example `"Principles of Programming Languages"`.

Table 1.3 Character strings in Java

In Caml, variable declaration is written as `let x = ref t in p` *and it isn't necessary to explicitly declare the variable's type. It is not possible in Caml to declare a variable without giving it an initial value.*

In C, like in Java, declaration is written `{T x = t; p}`. *It is possible to declare a variable without giving it an initial value, and in this case, it could have any value.*

In Java and in C, it is impossible to declare the same variable twice, and the following program is not valid.

```
int y - 4;
int x = 5;
int x = 6;
y = x;
```

In contrast, nothing in Caml stops you from writing

```
let y = ref 4
in let x = ref 5
in let x = ref 6
in y := !x
```

and this program assigns the value 6 *to the variable* y, *so it is the most recent declaration of* x *that is used. We say that the first declaration of* x *is* hidden *by the second.*

Java, Caml and C allow the creation of variables with an initial value that can never be changed. This type of variable is called a *constant* variable. A variable that is not constant is called a *mutable* variable. Java assumes that all variables are mutable unless you specify otherwise. To declare a constant variable in Java, you precede the variable type with the keyword `final`, for example

```
final int x = 4;
y = x + 1;
```

The following statement is not valid, because an attempt is made to alter the value of a constant variable

```
final int x = 4;
x = 5;
```

In Caml, to indicate that the variable x *is a constant variable, write* let x = t in p *instead of writing* let x = ref t in p. *When using constant variables, you do not write* !x *to express its value, but simply* x. *So, you can write* let x = 4 in y := x + 1, *while the statement* let x = 4 in x := 5 *is invalid. In C, you indicate that a variable is a constant variable by preceding its type with the keyword* const.

1.1.3 Sequence

A *sequence* is a construct that allows a single statement to be created out of two statements p_1 and p_2. In Java, a sequence is written as $\{p_1 \ p_2\}$. The statement $\{p_1 \ \{p_2 \ \{ \ \ldots \ p_n\} \ \ldots\}\}$ can also be written as $\{p_1 \ p_2 \ \ldots \ p_n\}$.

To execute the statement $\{p_1 \ p_2\}$ in the state s, the statement p_1 is first executed in the state s, which produces a new state s'. Then the statement p_2 is executed in the state s'.

In Caml, a sequence is written as p_1; p_2. *In C, it is written the same as it is in Java.*

1.1.4 Test

A *test* is a construct that allows the creation of a statement composed of a
boolean expression b and two statements p₁ and p₂. In Java, this statement is
written if (b) p₁ else p₂.

To execute the statement if (b) p₁ else p₂ in a state s, the value of
expression b is first computed in the state s, and depending on whether or not
its value is true or false, the statement p₁ or p₂ is executed in the state s.

In Caml, this statement is written if b then p₁ else p₂. *In C, it is written as it is in Java.*

1.1.5 Loop

A *loop* is a construct that allows the creation of a statement composed of a
boolean expression b and a statement p. In Java, this statement is written
while (b) p.

To execute the statement while (b) p in the state s, the value of b is first
computed in the state s. If this value is false, execution of this statement is
terminated. If the value is true, the statement p is executed, and the value
of b is recomputed in the new state. If this value is false, execution of this
statement is terminated. If the value is true, the statement p is executed, and
the value of b is recomputed in the new state... This process continues until b
evaluates to false.

This construct introduces a new possible behaviour: *non-termination*. Indeed, if the boolean value b always evaluates to true, the statement p will
continue to be executed forever, and the statement while (b) p will never
terminate. This is the case with the instruction

```
int x = 1;
while (x >= 0) {x = 3;}
```

To understand what is happening, imagine a fictional statement called
skip; that performs no action when executed. You can then define the statement while (b) p as shorthand for the statement

```
if (b) {p if (b) {p if (b) {p if (b) ...
                                  else skip;}
                          else skip;}
              else skip;}
      else skip;
```

So a loop is one of the ways in which you can express an infinite object using a finite expression. And the fact that a loop may fail to terminate is a consequence of the fact that it is an infinite object.

In Caml, this statement is written while b do p. *In C, it is written as it is in Java.*

1.2 Input and Output

An input construct allows a language to read values from a keyboard and other input devices, such as a mouse, disk, a network interface card, etc. An output construct allows values to be displayed on a screen and outputted to other peripherals, such as a printer, disk, a network interface card, etc.

1.2.1 Input

Input constructs in Java are fairly complex, so we will use an extension of Java created specially for this book: the class Ppl[1].

Evaluation of the expression Ppl.readInt() waits for the user to type a number on her/his keyboard, and returns this number as the value of the expression. A typical usage is n = Ppl.readInt();. The class Ppl also contains the construction Ppl.readDouble which allows decimal numbers to be read from the keyboard, and the construction Ppl.readChar which allows characters to be read.

1.2.2 Output

Execution of the statement System.out.print(t); outputs the value of expression t to the screen. Execution of the statement System.out.println(); outputs a newline character that moves the cursor to the next line. Execution of the statement System.out.println(t); outputs the value of expression t to the screen, followed by a newline character.

Exercise 1.2

Write a Java program that reads an integer n from the keyboard, computes the value of 2^n and outputs it to the screen.

---

[1] The file Ppl.java is available on the author's web site. Simply place it in the current directory to use the examples described here.

Exercise 1.3

> Write a Java program that reads an integer n from the keyboard, and
> outputs a boolean indicating whether the number is prime or not.

Graphical constructs that allow drawings to be displayed are fairly complex
in Java. But, the class `Ppl` contains some simple constructions to produce
graphics. The statement `Ppl.initDrawing(s,x,y,w,h);` creates a window
with the title `s`, of width `w` and of height `h`, positioned on the screen at coordinates `(x,y)`. The statement `Ppl.drawLine(x1,y1,x2,y2);` draws a line
segment with endpoints `(x1,y1)` and `(x2,y2)`. The statement `Ppl.drawCircle`
`(x,y,r);` draws a circle with centre `(x,y)` and with radius `r`. The statement `Ppl.paintCircle(x,y,r);` draws a filled circle and the statement
`Ppl.eraseCircle(x,y,r);` allows you to erase it.

1.3 The Semantics of the Imperative Core

We can, as we have below, express in English what happens when a statement
is executed. While this is possible for the simple examples in this chapter, such
explanations quickly become complicated and imprecise. Therefore, we shall
introduce a theoretical framework that might seem a bit too comprehensive at
first, but its usefulness will become clear shortly.

1.3.1 The Concept of a State

We define an infinite set `Var` whose elements are called *variables*. We also define
the set `Val` of *values* which are integers, booleans, etc. A *state* is a function that
associates elements of a finite subset of `Var` to elements of the set `Val`.

For example, the state $[x = 5, y = 6]$ associates the value 5 to the variable `x` and the value 6 to the variable `y`. On the set of states, we define an
update function + such that the state `s` + `(x = v)` is identical to the state `s`,
except for the variable `x`, which now becomes associated with the value `v`. This
operation is always defined, whether `x` is originally in the domain of `s` or not.

We can then simply define a function called Θ, which for each pair `(t,s)`
composed of an expression `t` and a state `s`, produces the value of this expression
in this state. For example, $\Theta(x + 3, [x = 5, y = 6]) = 8$.

This is a partial function, because a state is a function with a finite domain
while the set of variables is infinite. For example, the expression `z + 3` has no

value in the state [x = 5, y = 6]. In practice, this means that attempting to compute the value of the expression z + 3 in the state [x = 5, y = 6] produces an error.

Executing a statement within a state produces another state, and we define what happens when a statement is executed using a function called Σ. Σ has a statement p, an initial state s and produces a new state, Σ(p,s). This is also a partial function. Σ(p,s) is undefined when executing the statement p in the state s produces an error or does not terminate.

In the case of a statement p having the form x = t;, the Σ function is defined as follows

$$\Sigma(\text{x = t;},\text{s}) = \text{s} + (\text{x} = \Theta(\text{t,s})).$$

For example, Σ(x = x + 1;,[x = 5]) = [x = 6]. This is equivalent to saying 'Executing the statement x = t; loads the memory location x with the value of expression t'.

1.3.2 Decomposition of the State

A state s is a function that maps a finite subset of Var to the set Val. It will be helpful for the next chapter if we decompose this function as the composition of two other functions of finite domains: the first is known as the *environment*, which maps a finite subset of the set Var to an intermediate set Ref, whose elements are called *references* and the second, is called the *memory state*, which maps a finite subset of the set Ref to the set Val.

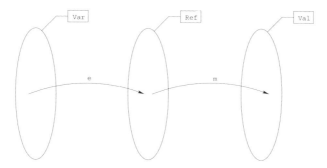

This brings us to propose two infinite sets, Var and Ref, and a set Val of values. The set of *environments* is defined as the set of functions that map a finite subset of the set Var to the set Ref. The set of *memory states* is defined as the set of functions mapping a finite subset of the set Ref to the set Val. For the set of environments, we define an update function + such that the environment e + (x = r) is identical to e, except at x, which now becomes associated with

the reference r. For the set of memory states, we define an update function +
such that the memory state m + (r = v) is identical to m, except at r, which
now becomes associated with the value v.

However, constant variables complicate things a little bit. For one, the environment must keep track of which variables are constant and which are mutable.
So, we define an environment to be a function mapping a finite subset of the
set Var to the set {constant, mutable} × Ref. We will, however, continue
to write e(x) to mean the reference associated to x in the environment e.

Then, at the point of execution of the declaration of a constant variable
x, we directly associate the variable to a value in the environment, instead of
associating it to a reference which is then associated to a value in the memory state. The idea is that the memory state contains information that can be
modified by an assignment, while the environment contains information that
cannot. To avoid having a target set for the environment function that is overly
complicated, we propose that Ref is a subset of Val, which brings us to propose that the environment is a function that maps a finite subset of Var to
{constant, mutable} × Val and the memory state is a function that maps
a finite subset of Ref to Val.

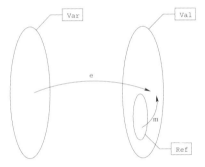

1.3.3 A Visual Representation of a State

It can be helpful to visualise states with a diagram. Each reference is represented
with a box. Two boxes placed in different positions always refer to separate
references.

Then, we represent the environment by adding one or more labels to certain
references.

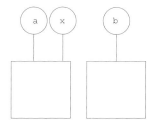

Even though each label is associated with a unique reference, nothing prevents two labels from being associated with the same reference, since an environment is a function, but not necessarily an injective function. Finally, we represent the memory state by filling each square with a value.

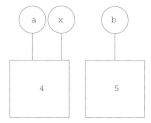

When a variable is associated directly with a value in the environment, we do not draw a box and we put the label directly on the value.

1.3.4 The Value of Expressions

The function Θ now associates a value to each triplet composed of an expression, an environment, and a memory state. For example, Θ(x + 3,[x = r_1, y = r_2],[r_1 = 5, r_2 = 6]) = 8.

For Java, this function is then defined as

– Θ(x,e,m) = m(e(x)), if x is a mutable variable in e,

– Θ(x,e,m) = e(x), if x is a constant variable in e,

– Θ(c,e,m) = c, if c is a constant, such as 4, true, etc.,

– Θ(t + u,e,m) = Θ(t,e,m) + Θ(u,e,m),

– Θ(t - u,e,m) = Θ(t,e,m) - Θ(u,e,m),

$- \; \Theta(\mathtt{t \; * \; u},\mathtt{e},\mathtt{m}) \; = \; \Theta(\mathtt{t},\mathtt{e},\mathtt{m}) \; * \; \Theta(\mathtt{u},\mathtt{e},\mathtt{m}),$

$- \; \Theta(\mathtt{t \; / \; u},\mathtt{e},\mathtt{m}) \; = \; \Theta(\mathtt{t},\mathtt{e},\mathtt{m}) \; / \; \Theta(\mathtt{u},\mathtt{e},\mathtt{m}),$

$- \; \Theta(\mathtt{t \; \% \; u},\mathtt{e},\mathtt{m}) \; = \; \Theta(\mathtt{t},\mathtt{e},\mathtt{m}) \; \% \; \Theta(\mathtt{u},\mathtt{e},\mathtt{m}),$

$-$ if $\Theta(\mathtt{b},\mathtt{e},\mathtt{m})$ = `true` then

$$\Theta((\mathtt{b}) \; ? \; \mathtt{t} \; : \; \mathtt{u},\mathtt{e},\mathtt{m}) \; = \; \Theta(\mathtt{t},\mathtt{e},\mathtt{m}),$$

if $\Theta(\mathtt{b},\mathtt{e},\mathtt{m})$ = `false` then

$$\Theta((\mathtt{b}) \; ? \; \mathtt{t} \; : \; \mathtt{u},\mathtt{e},\mathtt{m}) \; = \; \Theta(\mathtt{u},\mathtt{e},\mathtt{m}).$$

At first glance, this definition may seem circular, since to define the value of an expression of the form `t + u`, we use the value of expressions `t` and `u`. But the size of these expressions is smaller than that of `t + u`. This definition is therefore a definition by induction on the size of expressions.

The first clause of this definition indicates that the value of an expression that is a mutable variable is `m(e(x))`. We apply the function `e` to the variable `x`, which produces a reference, and the function `m` to this reference, which produces a value. If the variable is a constant variable, on the other hand, we find its value directly in the environment.

The definition of the function Θ for Caml is identical, except in the case of variables, where we have the unique clause

$- \; \Theta(\mathtt{x},\mathtt{e},\mathtt{m}) \; = \; \mathtt{e(x)},$

where the variable `x` is either mutable or constant.

For example, if `e` is the environment `[x = r]` and `m` is the memory state `[r = 4]` and that the variable `x` is mutable in `e`, the value $\Theta(\mathtt{x},\mathtt{e},\mathtt{m})$ is 4 in Java, but is `r` in Caml.

Caml also has a construct `!` such that

$- \; \Theta(\mathtt{!t},\mathtt{e},\mathtt{m}) \; = \; \mathtt{m}(\Theta(\mathtt{t},\mathtt{e},\mathtt{m})).$

If `x` is a variable, then the value of `!x` is $\Theta(\mathtt{!x},\mathtt{e},\mathtt{m}) = \mathtt{m}(\Theta(\mathtt{x},\mathtt{e},\mathtt{m})) = \mathtt{m(e(x))}$ that is the value of `x` in Java. This explains why we write `y := !x + 1` in Caml, where we write `y = x + 1;` in Java.

In Caml, references that can be associated to an integer in memory are of the type `int ref`. For example, the variable `x` and the value `r` from this example are of the type `int ref`. In contrast to the variable `x`, the expressions `!x`, `!x + 1`, ... are of the type `int`.

The definition of the function Θ for C is the same as the definition used for Java.

Exercise 1.4

Give the definition of the function Θ for expressions of the form t & u and t | u.

Unlike the boolean operator & that evaluates its two arguments, the operator && evaluates its second argument only if the first argument evaluates to true. Give the definition of the function Θ for expressions of the form t && u.

Answer the same question for the boolean operator ||, which only evaluates its second argument if the first argument evaluates to false.

1.3.5 Execution of Statements

The function Σ now associates memory states to triplets composed of an instruction, an environment, and a memory state. The function Σ in Java is defined below.

– When the statement p is a mutable variable declaration of the form {T x = t; q}, the function Σ is defined as follows

$$\Sigma(\{T\ x\ =\ t;\ q\}, e, m)\ =\ \Sigma(q, e\ +\ (x\ =\ r), m\ +\ (r\ =\ \Theta(t, e, m)))$$

where r is a new reference that does not appear in e or m.

– When the statement p is a constant variable declaration of the form {final T x = t; q}, the function Σ is defined as follows

$$\Sigma(\{final\ T\ x\ =\ t;\ q\}, e, m)\ =\ \Sigma(q, e\ +\ (x\ =\ \Theta(t, e, m)), m).$$

– When the statement p is an assignment of the form x = t;, the function is defined as follows

$$\Sigma(x\ =\ t;, e, m)\ =\ m\ +\ (e(x)\ =\ \Theta(t, e, m)).$$

– When the statement p is a sequence of the form {p_1 p_2}, the function Σ is defined as follows

$$\Sigma(\{p_1\ p_2\}, e, m)\ =\ \Sigma(p_2, e, \Sigma(p_1, e, m)).$$

– When the statement p is a test of the form if (b) p_1 else p_2, the function Σ is defined as follows. If $\Theta(b, e, m)$ = true then

$$\Sigma(\texttt{if (b) p}_1 \texttt{ else p}_2\texttt{,e,m}) = \Sigma(\texttt{p}_1\texttt{,e,m}).$$

If $\Theta(\texttt{b,e,m}) = \texttt{false}$ then

$$\Sigma(\texttt{if (b) p}_1 \texttt{ else p}_2\texttt{,e,m}) = \Sigma(\texttt{p}_2\texttt{,e,m}).$$

— This brings us to the case where the statement p is a loop of the form while
  (b) q. We have seen that introducing the imaginary statement skip; such
  that $\Sigma(\texttt{skip;,e,m}) = \texttt{m}$, we can define the statement while (b) q as a
  shorthand for the infinite statement

```
if (b) {q if (b) {q if (b) {q if (b) ...
                                 else skip;}
                      else skip;}
              else skip;}
      else skip;
```

When dealing with these types of infinite constructs, we often try to approach them as limits of finite approximations. We therefore introduce an
imaginary statement called giveup; such that the function Σ is never defined on (giveup;,e,m). We can define a sequence of finite approximations
of the statement while (b) q.

$\texttt{p}_0$ = if (b) giveup; else skip;

$\texttt{p}_1$ = if (b) {q if (b) giveup; else skip;} else skip;

...

$\texttt{p}_{n+1}$ = if (b) {q $\texttt{p}_n$} else skip;.

The statement $\texttt{p}_n$ tries to execute the statement while (b) q by completing
a maximum of n complete trips through the loop. If, after n loops, it has not
terminated on its own, it gives up.

If isn't hard to prove that for every integer n and state e, m, if $\Sigma(\texttt{p}_n\texttt{,e,m})$
is defined, then for all n' greater than n, $\Sigma(\texttt{p}_{n'}\texttt{,e,m})$ is also defined, and
$\Sigma(\texttt{p}_{n'}\texttt{,e,m}) = \Sigma(\texttt{p}_n\texttt{,e,m})$. This formalises the fact that if the statement
while (b) q terminates when the maximum number of loops is n, then it
also terminates, and to the same state, when the maximum number of loops
is n'.

There are therefore two possibilities for the sequence $\Sigma(\texttt{p}_n\texttt{,e,m})$: either it is
never defined, or it is defined beyond a certain point, and in this case, it is
constant over its domain. In the second case, we call the value it takes over
its domain the *limit* of the sequence. In contrast, the sequence does not have

a limit if it is never defined. We can now define the function Σ in the case where the statement p is of the form while (b) q

$$\Sigma(\texttt{while (b) q},e,m) = \lim_n \Sigma(p_n,e,m).$$

Note that the statements p_i are not always shorter than p, but if p contains k nested while loops, p_i contains k - 1. The definition of the function Σ is thus a double induction on the number of nested while loops, and on the size of the statement.

Exercise 1.5

What is the memory state $\Sigma(\texttt{x = 7;},[\texttt{x = r}],[\texttt{r = 5}])$?

The definition of the function Σ for Caml is not very different from the definition used for Java. In Caml, any expression that evaluates to a reference can be placed to the left of the sign :=, while in Java, only a variable can appear to the left of the sign =. The value of the function Σ of Caml for the statement t := u *is defined below:*

$-\ \Sigma(\texttt{t := u},e,m) = m + (\Theta(t,e,m) = \Theta(u,e,m))$

In the case where the expression t *is a variable* x*, we have* $\Sigma(\texttt{x := u},e,m)$ *= m + ($\Theta(x,e,m) = \Theta(u,e,m)$) = m + (e(x) = $\Theta(u,e,m)$) and we end up with the same definition of Σ used for Java.*

The definition of the function Σ for C is not very different from the definition used for Java. The main difference is in case of variable declaration

$$\Sigma(\{\texttt{T x = t; q}\},e,m) = (\Sigma(q,e+(x=r),m + (r = \Theta(t,e,m))))_{|\text{Ref}-\{r\}}$$

where r *is a new reference that does not appear in* e *or* m*, and the notation* $m_{|\text{Ref}-\{r\}}$ *designates the memory state* m *in which we have removed the ordered pair* r = v *if it existed. Thus, if we execute the statement* {int x = 4; p} q *in the state* e*,* m*, we execute the statement* p *in the state* e + (x = r)*,* m + (r = 4) *in C as in Java. In contrast, we execute the statement* q *in the state* e*,* m + (r = 4) *in Java and in the state* e*,* m *in C.*

As, in the environment e*, there is no variable that allows the reference* r *to be accessed, the ordered pair* r = 4 *no longer serves a purpose sitting in memory. Thus, whether it is is left alone, as in Java or Caml, or deleted, as in C, is immaterial. However, we will see, in Exercise 2.17, that this choice in C is a source of difficulty when the language contains other constructs.*

Exercise 1.6

The *incomplete test* allows the creation of a statement composed of a boolean expression and a statement. This statement is written if (b) p. The value of the function Σ for this statement is defined as follows. If $\Theta(\texttt{b},e,m) = \texttt{true}$ then

$$\Sigma(\text{if (b) p,e,m}) = \Sigma(\text{p,e,m}).$$

If $\Theta(\text{b,e,m}) = \text{false}$ then

$$\Sigma(\text{if (b) p,e,m}) = \text{m}.$$

Show that it is possible to define this construct using a complete test and the statement `skip;`.

Exercise 1.7

The loop `do` allows the creation of a statement composed of a boolean expression and a statement. This statement is written `do p while (b)`. This is a shorthand of the statement `{p while (b) p}`. Give the definition of the function Σ for this construct.

Exercise 1.8

The loop `for` allows the creation of a statement composed of three statements and a boolean expression. This statement is written `for(p₁; b;` `p₂) p₃`. It is a shorthand for the statement `p₁; while (b) {p₃ p₂;}`. What does the following statement do?

```
{y = 1; for(x = 1; x <= 10; x = x + 1) y = y * x;}
```

Exercise 1.9

Give the definition of the Σ function for the declaration of a variable without an initial value.

Exercise 1.10

Imagine an environment `e` — which cannot be created in Java — $[\text{x} = \text{r}, \text{y} = \text{r}]$, `m`, the memory state $[\text{r} = 4]$, `p`, the statement `x = x + 1;`, and `m'`, the memory $\Sigma(\text{p,e,m})$. What is the value associated with `y` in the state `e`, `m'`? Answer the same question for the environment $[\text{x} = \text{r}_1, \text{y} = \text{r}_2]$ and memory $[\text{r}_1 = 4, \text{r}_2 = 4]$.

Draw these two states.

Exercise 1.11

Imagine that all memory states have a special reference: `out`. Define the function Σ for the output construct `System.out.print` from the Section 1.2.

Exercise 1.12

In this exercise, imagine a data type that allows integers to be of any size. To each statement `p` in the imperative core of Java, we associate the partial function from integers to integers that, to the integer n, associates the value associated to out in the memory state Σ(p,[x = in, y = out],[in = n, out = 0]).

A partial function f, from integers to integers, is called *computable* if there exists a statement p such that f is the function associated with p.

Show that there exists a function that is non computable.

Hint: use the fact that there does not exist a surjective function of $\mathbb{N}$ in the set of functions from $\mathbb{N}$ to $\mathbb{N}$.

2
Functions

2.1 The Concept of Functions

2.1.1 Avoiding Repetition

```
System.out.print("Flight ");
System.out.print("819");
System.out.print(" to ");
System.out.print("Tokyo");
System.out.print(" takes off at ");
System.out.println("8:50 AM");
System.out.println();
System.out.println();
System.out.println();

System.out.print("Flight ");
System.out.print("211");
System.out.print(" to ");
System.out.print("New York");
System.out.print(" takes off at ");
System.out.println("8:55 AM");
System.out.println();
System.out.println();
System.out.println();
```

G. Dowek, *Principles of Programming Languages,*
Undergraduate Topics in Computer Science, DOI 10.1007/978-1-84882-032-6_2,
© Springer-Verlag London Limited 2009

In this program, the block of three statements `System.out.println();`, which skips three lines, is repeated twice. Instead of repeating it there, you can define a *function* `jumpThreeLines`

```
static void jumpThreeLines () {
 System.out.println();
 System.out.println();
 System.out.println();}
```

And use it in the main program

```
System.out.print("Flight ");
System.out.print("819");
System.out.print(" to ");
System.out.print("Tokyo");
System.out.print(" takes off at ");
System.out.println("8:50 AM");
jumpThreeLines();

System.out.print("Flight ");
System.out.print("211");
System.out.print(" to ");
System.out.print("New York");
System.out.print(" takes off at ");
System.out.println("8:55 AM");
jumpThreeLines();
```

The statement `jumpThreeLines();` that is found in the main program is named the *call* of the function `jumpThreeLines`. The statement that is found in the function and that is executed on each call is named the *body* of the function.

Organising a program into functions allows you to avoid repeated code, or redundancy. As well, it makes programs clearer and easier to read: to understand the program above, it isn't necessary to understand how the function `jumpThreeLines();` is implemented; you only need to understand what it does. This also allows you to organise the structure of your program. You can choose to write the function `jumpThreeLines();` one day, and the main program another day. You can also organise a programming team, where one programmer writes the function `jumpThreeLines();`, and another writes the main program.

This mechanism is similar to that of mathematical definitions that allows you to use the word 'group' instead of always having to say 'A set closed under an associative operation with an identity, and where every element has an inverse'.

2.1.2 Arguments

Some programming languages, like assembly and Basic, have only a simple function mechanism, like the one above. But the example above demonstrates that this mechanism isn't sufficient for eliminating redundancy, as the main program is composed of two nearly identical segments. It would be nice to place these segments into a function. But to deal with the difference between these two copies, we must introduce three parameters: one for the flight number, one for the destination and one for the take off time. We can now define the function `takeOff`

```
static void takeOff
            (final String n, final String d, final String t) {
System.out.print("Flight ");
System.out.print(n);
System.out.print(" to ");
System.out.print(d);
System.out.print(" takes off at ");
System.out.print(t);
System.out.println();
System.out.println();
System.out.println();}
```

and to use it in the main program, we write

```
takeOff("819","Tokyo","8:50 AM");
takeOff("211","New York","8:55 AM");
```

The variables n, d and t which are listed as arguments in the function's definition, are called *formal arguments* of the function. When we call the function `takeOff("819","Tokyo","8:50 AM");` the expressions "819", "Tokyo" and "8:50 AM" that are given as arguments are called the *real arguments* of the call.

A formal argument, like any variable, can be declared constant or mutable. If it is constant, it cannot be altered inside the body of the function.

To follow up the comparison, mathematical language also uses parameters in definitions: 'The group $\mathbb{Z}/n\mathbb{Z}$ is ...', 'A K-vector space is ...', ...

In Caml, a function declaration is written `let f x y ... = t in p.`

```
let takeOff n d t =
   print_string "Flight ";
   print_string n;
   print_string " to ";
   print_string d;
```

```
    print_string " takes off at ";
    print_string t;
    print_newline ();
    print_newline ();
    print_newline ()
in takeOff "819" "Tokyo" "8:50 AM";
    takeOff "211" "New York" "8:55 AM"
```

Formal arguments are always constant variables. However, if the argument itself is a reference, you can assign to it, just like to any other reference.

In C, a function declaration is written as in Java, but without the keyword static.

2.1.3 Return Values

```
a = 3;
b = 4;
c = 5;
d = 12;
u = Math.sqrt(a * a + b * b);
v = Math.sqrt(c * c + d * d);
```

In this program, we want to isolate the computation Math.sqrt(x * x + y * y) in a function called hypotenuse. But in contrast to the function takeOff that performs output, the hypotenuse function must compute a value and send it back to the main program. This return value is the inverse of argument passing that sends values from the main program to the body of the function. The type of the returned value is written before the name of the function. The function hypotenuse, for example, is declared as follows.

```
static double hypotenuse (final double x, final double y) {
  return Math.sqrt(x * x + y * y);}
```

And the main program is written as follows.

```
a = 3;
b = 4;
c = 5;
d = 12;
u = hypotenuse(a,b);
v = hypotenuse(c,d);
```

In Caml, the function hypotenuse *is written*

```
let hypotenuse x y = sqrt(x *. x +. y *. y)
```

In C, the function hypotenuse *is written as in Java, but without the keyword* static *and using C's square root function which is written as* sqrt *instead of* Math.sqrt.

2.1.4 The return Construct

As we have seen, in Caml, the function hypotenuse is written

```
let hypotenuse x y = sqrt(x *. x +. y *. y)
```

In Java and in C, in contrast, you must precede the return value with the keyword return. So, in Java, instead of writing

```
static double hypotenuse (final double x, final double y) {
 Math.sqrt(x * x + y * y);}
```

you should write

```
static double hypotenuse (final double x, final double y) {
 return Math.sqrt(x * x + y * y);}
```

When return occurs in the middle of the function instead of the end, it stops the execution of the function. So, instead of writing

```
static int sign (final int x) {
 if (x < 0) return -1;
 else if (x == 0) return 0;
 else return 1;}
```

you can write

```
static int sign (final int x) {
 if (x < 0) return -1;
 if (x == 0) return 0;
 return 1;}
```

Basically, if the value of x is negative, the statement return -1; interrupts the execution of the function, and the other two statements will not be executed.

Exercise 2.1

In Java, write a function that takes an integer argument called n and returns the integer 2^n.

Exercise 2.2

In Java, write a function that takes an integer argument called n and returns a boolean that indicates whether n is prime or not.

2.1.5 Functions and Procedures

A function can on one hand cause an action to be performed, such as outputting a value or altering memory, and on the other hand can return a value. Functions that do not return a value are called *procedures*.

In some languages, like Pascal, procedures are differentiated from functions using a special keyword. In Caml, a procedure is simply a function that returns a value of type `unit`. Like its name implies, `unit` is a singleton type that contains only one value, written `()`. In Caml, a procedure always returns the value `()`, which communicates no information.

Java and C lie somewhere in the middle, because we declare a procedure in these languages by replacing the return type by the keyword `void`. In contrast to the type `unit` of Caml, there is no actual type `void` in Java and C. For example, you cannot declare a variable of type `void`.

A function call, such as `hypotenuse(a,b)`, is an expression, while a procedure call, such as `takeOff("819","Tokyo","8:50 AM");`, is a statement.

There are however certain nuances to consider, because a function call can also be a statement. You can, for example, write the statement `hypotenuse(a,b);`. The value returned by the function is simply discarded. However, even if a language allows it, using functions in this way is considered to be bad form. The Caml compilers, for example, will produce a warning in this case.

In Java and in C, a procedure, that is to say a function with return type of `void` cannot be used as an expression. For example, to write

```
x = takeOff("819","Tokyo","8:50 AM");
```

the variable `x` would have to be of the type `void` and we have seen that there is no such variable. In Caml, in contrast, a procedure is nothing but a function with a return type `unit` and you can easily write

```
x := takeOff("819","Tokyo","8:50 AM")
```

if the variable `x` is of type `unit ref`. However, if such an assignment is possible, it is not useful.

In general, no matter what the language, it is considered good form to separate functions and procedures. Functions return a value, and do not perform actions such as outputting a value, and are used as expressions. Procedures do not return a value, can perform actions, and are used as statements.

2.1.6 Global Variables

Imagine that we would like to isolate the statement x = 0; with a function in
the program

```
int x;
x = 3;
x = 0;
```

We then would write the function

```
static void reset () {x = 0;}
```

and the main program

```
int x;
x = 3;
reset();
```

But this program is not correct, as the statement x = 0; is no longer in the
scope of variable x. For the function reset to have access to the variable x, you
must declare a variable x as a *global* variable, and the access to this variable is
given to all the functions as well as to the main program

```
static int x;
```

```
static void reset () {x = 0;}
```

and the main program

```
x = 3;
reset();
```

    All functions can use any global variable, whether they are declared before
or after the function.

2.1.7 The Main Program

A *program* is composed of three main sections: global variable declarations x_1,
..., x_n, function declarations f_1, ..., $f_{n'}$, and the *main program* p which is a
statement.

    A program can thus be written as

```
static T₁ x₁ = t₁;
...
```

```
static Tₙ xₙ = tₙ;

static ... f₁ (...) ...
...
static ... fₙ′ (...) ...


p
```

However, in Java, the main program is placed inside a special function called:
`main`. The `main` function must not return a value, and must always have an
argument of type `String []`. In addition to the keyword `static`, the definition
of the `main` function must also be preceded by the keyword `public`.

In addition, the program must be given a name, which is given with the
keyword `class`. The general form of a program is:

```
class Prog {

  static T₁ x₁ = t₁;
  ...
  static Tₙ xₙ = tₙ;

  static ... f₁ (...) ...
  ...
  static ... fₙ′ (...) ...

  public static void main (String [] args) {p}}
```

   For example
```
class Hypotenuse {

  static double hypotenuse (final double x, final double y) {
    return Math.sqrt(x * x + y * y);}

  public static void main (String [] args) {
    System.out.println(hypotenuse(3,4));}}
```

   In Caml, there is no main *function and the syntax of the language separates*
functions from the main program

```
let hypotenuse x y = sqrt(x *. x +. y *. y)
in print_float(hypotenuse 3.0 4.0)
```

In C, the main program is also a function called main. *For historical reasons, the* main *function must always return an integer, and is usually terminated with* return 0;. *You don't give a name to the program itself, so a program is simply a series of global variable and function declarations.*

```
double hypotenuse (const double x, const double y) {
 return sqrt(x * x + y * y);}


int main () {
 printf("%f\n",hypotenuse(3,4));
 return 0;}
```

2.1.8 Global Variables Hidden by Local Variables

```
class Prog {

 static int n;

 static int f (final int x) {
  int p = 5;
  return n + p + x;}

 static int g (final int x) {
  int n = 5;
  return n + n + x;}

 public static void main (String [] args) {
  n = 4;
  System.out.println(f(6));
  System.out.println(g(6));}}
```

The value of the expression f(6) is 15. The function f adds the global variable n, which has been initialised to 4 in the main program, the local variable p, with a value of 5, and the argument x, with a value of 6.

In contrast, the value of the expression g(6) is 16, because both occurrences of n refer to the local variable n, which has a value of 5. In the environment in which the body of function g is executed, the global variable n is hidden by the local variable n and is no longer accessible.

2.1.9 Overloading

In Java, it is impossible to define two functions with the same name, for example

```
static int f (final int x) {
 return x;}
```

```
static int f (final int x) {
 return x + 1;}
```

except when the number or types of their arguments are different. You can, for example, declare three identically named functions

```
static int f (final int x) {
 return x;}
```

```
static int f (final int x, final int y) {
 return x + 1;}
```

```
static int f (final boolean x) {
 return 7;}
```

At the time of evaluation of an expression of the form $f(t_1, \ldots, t_n)$, the called function is chosen based on its name as well as the number and types of its arguments. The expressions $f(4)$, $f(4,2)$, and $f(true)$ evaluate to 4, 5, and 7 respectively. In this case, we say that the name f is *overloaded*.

There is no overloading in Caml. The programs

```
let f x = x in let f x = x + 1 in print_int (f 4)
```

and

```
let f x = x in let f x y = x + 1 in print_int (f 4 2)
```

are valid, but the first declaration is simply hidden by the second.

There is also no overloading in C, and the program

```
int f (const int x) {return x;}
int f (const int x, const int y) {return x + 1;}
...
```

is invalid.

2.2 The Semantics of Functions

This brings us to extend the definition of the Σ function. In addition to a statement, an environment, and a memory state, the Σ function now also takes an argument called the *global environment* G. This global environment comprises an environment called e that contains global variables and a function of a finite domain that associates each function name with its definition, that is to say with its formal arguments and the body of the function to be executed at each call.

We must then take into account the fact that, because functions can modify memory, the evaluation of an expression can now modify memory as well. Because of this fact, the result of the evaluation of an expression, when it exists, is no longer simply a value, but an ordered pair composed of a value and a memory state.

Also, we must explain what happens when the statement return is executed, in particular the fact that the execution of this statement interrupts the execution of the body of the function.

This brings us to reconsider the definition of the function Σ in the case of the sequence

$$\Sigma(\{p_1\ p_2\}, e, m, G) = \Sigma(p_2, e, \Sigma(p_1, e, m, G), G)$$

according to which executing the sequence $\{p_1\ p_2\}$ consists of executing p_1 and then p_2.

Indeed, if p_1 is of the form return t;, or more generally if the execution of p_1 causes the execution of return, then the statement p_2 will not be executed. We will therefore consider that the result $\Sigma(p_1, e, m, G)$ of the execution of p_1 in the state e, m is not simply a memory state, but a more complex object. One part of this object is a boolean value that indicates if the execution of p_1 has occurred normally, or if a return statement was encountered. If the execution occurred normally, the second part of this object is the memory state produced by this execution. If the statement return was encountered, the second part of this object is composed of the return value and the memory state produced by the execution. From now on, the target set of the Σ function will be ({normal} × Mem) ∪ ({return} × Val × Mem) where Mem is the set of memory states, that is to say the set of functions that map a finite subset of Ref to the set Val.

Finally, we should also take into account the fact that a function cannot only be called from the main program — the main function — but also from inside another function. However, we will discuss this topic later.

2.2.1 The Value of Expressions

The evaluation function of an expression is now defined as

- Θ(x,e,m,G) = (m(e(x)),m), if x is a mutable variable in e,

- Θ(x,e,m,G) = (e(x),m), if x is a constant variable in e,

- Θ(c,e,m,G) = (c,m), if c is a constant,

- Θ(t $\otimes$ u,e,m,G) = (v $\otimes$ w,m'') where $\otimes$ is an arithmetical or logical operation, (v,m') = Θ(t,e,m,G) and (w,m'') = Θ(u,e,m',G),

- if Θ(b,e,m,G) = (true,m') then

$$\Theta((b) \ ? \ t \ : \ u,e,m,G) = \Theta(t,e,m',G),$$

if Θ(b,e,m,G) = (false,m') then

$$\Theta((b) \ ? \ t \ : \ u,e,m,G) = \Theta(u,e,m',G).$$

- Θ(f(t$_1$,...,t$_n$),e,m,G) is defined this way.

Let x_1, ..., x_n be the list of formal arguments and p the body of the function associated with the name f in G. Let e' be the environment of global variables of G. Let (v$_1$,m$_1$) = Θ(t$_1$,e,m,G), (v$_2$,m$_2$) = Θ(t$_2$,e,m$_1$,G), ..., (v$_n$,m$_n$) = Θ(t$_n$,e,m$_{n-1}$,G) be the result of the evaluation of real arguments t_1, ..., t_n of the function.

For the formal mutable arguments x_i, we consider arbitrary distinct references r_i that do not appear either in e' or in m$_n$. We define the environment e'' = e' + (x$_1$ = v$_1$) + (x$_2$ = r$_2$) + ... + (x$_n$ = r$_n$) in which we associate the formal argument x_i to the value v_i or to the reference r_i according to whether it is constant or mutable, and the memory state m'' = m$_n$ + (r$_2$ = v$_2$) + ... + (r$_n$ = v$_n$) in which we associate to the values v_i the references r_i associated to formal mutable arguments.

Consider the object Σ(p,e'',m'',G) obtained by executing the body of the function in the state formed by the environment e'' and the memory state m''. If this object is of the form (return,v,m''') then we let

$$\Theta(f(t_1,...,t_n),e,m,G) = (v,m''').$$

Otherwise, the function Θ is not defined: the evaluation of the expression produces an error because the evaluation of the body of the function has not encountered a return statement.

2.2.2 Execution of Statements

We now define what occurs when a statement is executed.

- When the statement p is a declaration of the form {T x = t; p} or {final T x = t; p}, if $\Theta(t,e,m,G) = (v,m')$ then

$$\Sigma(\{T\ x\ =\ t;\ p\},e,m,G)\ =\ \Sigma(p,e\ +\ (x\ =\ r),m'\ +\ (r\ =\ v),G)$$

where r is an arbitrary reference that does not appear in e and m, and

$$\Sigma(\{final\ T\ x\ =\ t;\ p\},e,m,G)\ =\ \Sigma(p,e\ +\ (x\ =\ v),m',G).$$

- When the statement p is an assignment of the form x = t;, if $\Theta(t,e,m,G) = (v,m')$ then

$$\Sigma(x\ =\ t;,e,m,G)\ =\ (normal,m'\ +\ (e(x)\ =\ v)).$$

- When the statement p is a sequence of the form $\{p_1\ p_2\}$, if $\Sigma(p_1,e,m,G) = (normal,m')$ then

$$\Sigma(\{p_1\ p_2\},e,m,G)\ =\ \Sigma(p_2,e,m',G)$$

and if $\Sigma(p_1,e,m,G) = (return,v,m')$ then

$$\Sigma(\{p_1\ p_2\},e,m,G)\ =\ (return,v,m').$$

- When the statement p is a test of the form if (b) p_1 else p_2, if $\Theta(b,e,m,G) = (true,m')$ then

$$\Sigma(if\ (b)\ p_1\ else\ p_2,e,m,G)\ =\ \Sigma(p_1,e,m',G)$$

and if $\Theta(b,e,m,G) = (false,m')$ then

$$\Sigma(if\ (b)\ p_1\ else\ p_2,e,m,G)\ =\ \Sigma(p_2,e,m',G).$$

- The definition for loops is unchanged

$$\Sigma(while\ (b)\ q,e,m,G)\ =\ \lim_n\ \Sigma(p_n,e,m,G)$$

where

p_0 = if (b) giveup; else skip;

and p_{n+1} = if (b) {q p_n} else skip;.

– When the statement p is of the form `return t;`, if Θ(`t,e,m,G`) = (`v,m'`) then

$$\Sigma(\texttt{return t;,e,m,G}) = (\texttt{return,v,m'}).$$

– Finally, we add the case of functions, which is very similar to the case of functions in the definition of the evaluation of expressions, except that if the object Σ(`p,e'',m'',G`) has the form (`normal,m'''`), then we let

$$\Sigma(\texttt{f(t}_1\texttt{,...,t}_n\texttt{);,e,m,G}) = (\texttt{normal,m'''})$$

and if it has the form (`return,v,m'''`), we let

$$\Sigma(\texttt{f(t}_1\texttt{,...,t}_n\texttt{);,e,m,G}) = (\texttt{normal,m'''})$$

by ignoring the value v: we have the case where a function is used as a statement.

For example, when we execute the statement `u = hypotenuse(a,b);` in the environment e = [`a = `r_1`, b = `r_2`, u = `r_3], the memory state m = [r_1 = 3.0, r_2 = 4.0, r_3 = 0.0], and the global environment G composed of the environment e and the function declaration `hypotenuse: (x,y)`, `return Math.sqrt(x * x + y * y);`, we start by evaluating the expression `hypotenuse(a,b)`. To do so, we start by evaluating a and b, which produces the values 3.0 and 4.0, without changing the memory state. And we create an environment e'' = [`a = `r_1`, b = `r_2`, u = `r_3`, x = `r_4`, y = `r_5] and the memory state m'' = [r_1 = 3.0, r_2 = 4.0, r_3 = 0.0, r_4 = 3.0, r_5 = 4.0]

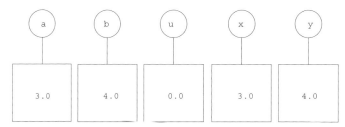

Next, we execute the body of the function, which produces the result (`return,5.0,m''`) and so Θ(`hypotenuse(a,b),e,m,G`) is (`5.0,m''`). The result of the execution of the statement `u = hypotenuse(a,b);` is then an ordered pair composed of a boolean `normal` and the memory state m'' = [r_1 = 3.0, r_2 = 4.0, r_3 = 5.0, r_4 = 3.0, r_5 = 4.0].

The value of the variable u in the state e, m''' is 5.0.

Exercise 2.3

What happens if the formal arguments x and y of the function hypotenuse are constant variables?

Exercise 2.4

What happens if you execute the statement u = hypotenuse(a,b);,
with the variables a, b, and u declared in the main function?

Finally, we can give the definition of the Σ function for the entire program.
Let P be a program formed of global variable declarations static T_1 a_1 = t_1;,
..., static T_n a_u = t_n; and of function declarations static U_1 f_1 (x_1) p_1;,
..., static $U_{n'}$ $f_{n'}$ ($x_{n'}$) $p_{n'}$;.

Let v_1, ..., v_n be the initial values given to global variables, that is to say the
values of expressions t_i. Let e be the environment [a_1 = v_1, a_2 = r_2, ...,
a_n = r_n] in which we associate the global variable a_i to the value v_i or to the
reference r_i whether it is constant or mutable, and m is the memory state [r_2
= v_2, ..., r_n = v_n], in which we associate the references r_i associated to
mutable global variables with the values v_i. Let G be the global environment
(e, [f_1 = (x_1,p_1), ..., $f_{n'}$ = ($x_{n'}$,$p_{n'}$)]).

The memory state Σ(P) is defined by

$$- \Sigma(P) = \Sigma(\text{main(null)};,e,m,G)$$

where null is a value of type String [] which we will discuss later.

Exercise 2.5

The function f is defined as follows

```
static int f (final int x) {
  int y = x;
  while (true) {
    y = y + 1;
    if (y == 1000) return y + 1;}}
```

What is returned from the function call f(500)?

Exercise 2.6

Imagine that all memory states contain two special references: in and
out. Write the definition of the function Σ for the input and output
constructs from Section 1.2.

2.2.3 Order of Evaluation

Since expressions can modify memory, consideration must be given to the fact that in the definition of Σ we have given, arguments of a function are evaluated from left to right. So, we evaluate t_1 in the memory state m, and t_2 in the memory state m_1 produced by the evaluation of t_1, ... So, the program

```
class Prog {

 static int n;

 static int f (final int x, final int y) {
  return x;}

 static int g (final int z) {
  n = n + z;
  return n;}

 public static void main (String [] args) {
  n = 0;
  System.out.println(f(g(2),g(7)));}}
```

outputs the result 2.

2.2.4 Caml

The definition of the function Σ for Caml is somewhat different from the definition of Σ used for Java. In Caml, all formal arguments are constant variables, so new references are never created at the point of a function call.

Also, in Caml, there is only one name space for functions and variables. In Java, the program

```
class Prog {

 static int f (final int x) {
  return x + 1;}

 static int f = 4;

 public static void main (String [] args) {
  System.out.println(f(f));}}
```

is valid, and in the expression `f(f)`, *the first occurrence of* `f` *is a function name* `f` *and the second occurrence of* `f` *is a variable name. In Caml, however, the program*

```
let f x = x + 1 in let f = 4 in print_int(f f)
```

is invalid. The function `f` *becomes hidden by the variable* `f`. *There is therefore no global environment: global variables and functions are declared in the environment, like variables. During the call of a function* `f`, *it is impossible to create the environment in which we must evaluate the body of the function using the global environment. Thus, in the environment, we must associate the name* `f`, *not only with the list of formal arguments and the body of the function, but also the environment to extend with the arguments for executing the body of the function. This environment is the environment in which the function is defined.*

So, the Java program

```
class Prog {

  static int f () {return x;}

  static int x = 4;

  public static void main (String [] args) {
    System.out.println(f ());}}
```

is valid, and outputs 4, *while the Caml program*

```
let f () = x in let x = 4 in print_int(f())
```

is invalid, because the variable `x` *in the body of* `f` *is not part of the environment of the definition of* `f`. *It is necessary to declare this variable before* `f`

```
let x = 4 in let f () = x in print_int(f())
```

Another difference is that the Caml compilers evaluate the arguments from right to left. For example, the program

```
let n = ref 0
in let f x y = x
in let g z = (n := !n + z; !n)
in print_int (f (g 2) (g 7))
```

results in 9 *and not* 2.

However, the definition of the Caml language does not specify the order of evaluation of the arguments of a function. Different compilers may evaluate arguments in a different order. It is up to the programmer to write programs whose result is not dependent on the order of evaluation.

Finally, there is no `return` *in Caml, and the result of the execution of a statement, like the evaluation of an expression, is an ordered pair composed of a value, possibly* `()`, *and a memory state.*

Exercise 2.7

Give the definition of the Σ function of Caml, assuming that arguments are always evaluated from right to left.

2.2.5 C

The definition of the Σ function for C is also somewhat different from the definition of Σ for Java.

In C, the references created at the moment of a function call are removed from the memory and the end of the execution of the body of the function.

Like in Caml, there is only one name space for functions and variables, and functions are declared in the same environment as variables. In this environment, we not only associate the name `f` *to the list of formal arguments and the body of the function, but also to the environment* `e` *to extend with the arguments for executing the body of the function. This environment is, like in Caml, the environment of the definition of the function. For example, the program*

```
int f () {return x;}

int x = 4;

int main () {
 printf("%d\n",f());
 return 0;}
```

is invalid.

C compilers also evaluate a function's arguments from left to right, as in Java. However, the definition of the language, like that of Caml, does not specify the order of evaluation of a function's arguments, and it is up to the programmer to write programs whose result does not depend on the order of evaluation.

Exercise 2.8

Give the definition of the Σ function for C, assuming that arguments are always evaluated from left to right.

2.3 Expressions as Statements

Now that we have defined the result of the evaluation of an expression as an ordered pair composed of a value and a state, we can better understand the link between expressions and statements.

In C, any expression followed by a semicolon is a statement. The value of an expression is simply ignored when it is used as a statement. If Θ(t,e,m,G) is the ordered pair (v,m') then Σ(t;,e,m,G) is the ordered pair composed of the boolean `normal` and the memory state m'. The situation is somewhat similar in Java, except that only certain expressions are eligible to be used as statements. For example, if f is a function, then f(t$_1$,...,t$_n$); is, as we have seen, a statement, but that is not the case with 1;. In Caml, there is no difference between statements and expressions, since statements are simply expressions of type `unit`.

Exercise 2.9

In Java and in C, the expression x = t assigns the value of t to x and returns this same value. How would you modify the definition of the Θ function to take into account expressions of this type? What is the output of the following program?

```
class Prog {

  public static void main (String [] args) {
    int x;
    int y;
    x = (y = 4);
    System.out.println(x);
    System.out.println(y);}}
```

2.4 Passing Arguments by Value and Reference

If the initial value of the variable x is 4 and that of the variable y is 7, after executing the statement {z = x; x = y; y = z;}, variable x has the value 7 and variable y has the value 4. More generally, this statement exchanges the values of these variables, using the *principle of the third glass*

Observe the behaviour of the following program

```
class Prog {

 static int a;

 static int b;

 static void swap (int x, int y) {int z; z = x; x = y; y = z;}

 static public void main (String [] args) {
  a = 4;
  b = 7;
  swap(a,b);
  System.out.println(a);
  System.out.println(b);}}
```

You might expect the values of a and b have been exchanged and that the numbers 7 and 4 are displayed, but surprisingly, the number 4 is displayed first, followed by the number 7.

In fact, this result is what is expected based on the definition of the Σ function given above. We start with an environment e = [a = r_1, b = r_2] and a memory state m = [r_1 = 4, r_2 = 7]. The call of the function swap(a,b); computes the values of the expressions a and b in the environment e and the memory state m. It obtains 4 and 7 respectively. Then, the environment [a = r_1, b = r_2, x = r_3, y = r_4] and the memory state [r_1 = 4, r_2 = 7, r_3 = 4, r_4 = 7] are created.

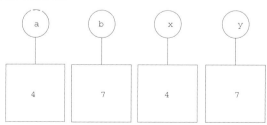

The values of the variables x and y are exchanged, which results in the memory state $[r_1 = 4, r_2 = 7, r_3 = 7, r_4 = 4, r_5 = 4]$ which returns control to the main program. The environment is then $e = [a = r_1, b = r_2]$ with the memory state $[r_1 = 4, r_2 = 7, r_3 = 7, r_4 = 4, r_5 = 4]$. The values of the variables a and b have not changed.

In other words, the function swap ignores the variables a and b. It can only use their value at the moment of the function call, and cannot modify their value: executing the statement swap(a,b); has the same result as executing the statement swap(4,7);.

The mechanism of argument passing that we have described is called *argument passing by value*. It does not allow the creation of a swap function that changes the contents of two variables. However, most programming languages have a construct that allows the creation of such a function. But, this construct is somewhat different in each language. Before seeing how this is done in Java, Caml, and C, we will look at the much simpler example of the Pascal language.

2.4.1 Pascal

The Pascal language has a built in calling mechanism to pass arguments by reference, *or* by variable. *In the definition of the* swap *procedure, we can precede each argument with the keyword* var.

```
procedure swap (var x : integer, var y : integer) ...
```

When an argument of a procedure or a function is declared using pass by reference, we can only apply this procedure or function to a variable. So, we can write swap(a,b) *but not* swap(4,7), *nor* swap(2 * a,b).

When we call the procedure swap(a,b), *instead of associating the variables* x *and* y *to new references assigning to these references the values of the procedure's arguments,* 4 *and* 7, *we associate the variables* x *and* y *to references associated with variables given as arguments to the procedure. So, we call the procedure* swap(a,b) *in an environment* $e = [a = r_1, b = r_2]$ *and a memory state* $m = [r_1 = 4, r_2 = 7]$, *instead of creating the environment* $[a = r_1, b = r_2, x = r_3, y = r_4]$ *and the memory state* $[r_1 = 4, r_2 = 7, r_3 = 4, r_4 = 7]$, *we create the environment* $[a = r_1, b = r_2, x = r_1, y = r_2]$ *while keeping the memory state* $[r_1 = 4, r_2 = 7]$.

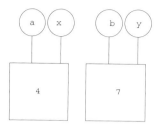

Because of this, the procedure `swap` *exchanges the contents of the references* r_1
and r_2 *and not of the references* r_3 *and* r_4

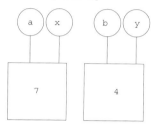

*and after execution of the procedure, the contents of the references associated
with the variables* a *and* b *have been exchanged.*

    *Being able to explain the mechanism of passing by reference is the main
motivation for decomposing the state into an environment and a memory state
by introducing an intermediate set of references, as we have done in the previous
chapter.*

Exercise 2.10

Give the definition of the Σ *function in the case of functions with an
argument passed by reference.*

2.4.2 Caml

*In Caml, passing by reference is not a primitive construct, but it can be accom-
plished by using the fact that references are also values.*

    For example, in the environment ⌈x = r⌉ *and in the memory state* [r =
4], *the value of the expression* !x *is the integer* 4, *but the value of the expression*
x *is the reference* r. *This allows the creation of a function* `swap` *that takes
two references as arguments and exchanges the values associated with these
references in the memory.*

```
let swap x y = let z = ref 0 in (z := !x; x := !y; y := !z)
```

    To exchange the values of the variables a *and* b, *you simply apply the func-
tion to the references* a *and* b *and not to the integers* !a *and* !b.

```
a:= 4;
b := 7;
swap a b;
print_int !a;
print_newline();
print_int !b;
print_newline()
```

Indeed, when we call the function swap a b *in the environment* [a = r_1, b = r_2] *and the memory state* [r_1 = 4, r_2 = 7], *we create the environment* [a = r_1, b = r_2, x – r_1, y = r_2] *in which the constant formal arguments* x *and* y *are linked to the real arguments* r_1 *and* r_2 *and we keep the same memory state* [r_1 = 4, r_2 = 7]

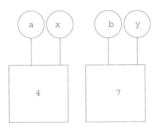

and the function swap *exchanges the contents of the references* r_1 *and* r_2 *and after the execution of the function, the contents of the references associated with the variables* a *and* b *have now also been exchanged.*

Exercise 2.11

What does the following program do?

```
let swap x y = let z = !x in (x := !y; y := z)
```

2.4.3 C

In C as well, the passing by reference is not a primitive construct, but it can be simulated by using a similar mechanism to that of Caml. The type of references that can be associated with a value of type T *in memory, written* T ref *in Caml, is written* T* *in C. The dereference construct, written* ! *in Caml, is written as* * *in C. For example, in the environment* [u = r_1] *and in the memory state* [r_1 = r_2, r_2 = 4], *the value of the expression* u *is the reference* r_2 *and the value of the expression* *u *is the integer* 4.

If x *is a variable, the reference associated with* x *in the environment, written simply as* x *in Caml, is written as* &x *in C. For example, in the environment*

[x = r] *and the memory state* [r = 4] *the value of expression* x *is the integer*
4, *the value of expression* &x *is the reference* r *and the value of expression* *&x
is the integer 4. *The* & *construct applies to a variable and not to an arbitrary
expression.*

Exercise 2.12

What does the following program output?

```
int main () {
 int x;
 int* u;

 x = 4;
 u = &x;
 printf("%d\n",*u);
 return 0;}
```

*Using these constructs, it becomes possible to create states in which some
references are associated with other references. It then becomes necessary to
update our graphical representation of states. When a memory state has a reference* r' *associated with a reference* r, *one solution is to write in the box of* r
the coordinates of the place where we have drawn the reference r' *on the page.
A better solution is to draw in the box of* r *an arrow that points to the reference*
r'.

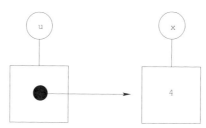

If t *is an expression of type* T* *then the language C has a new assignment
construct* *t = u;, *similar to the construct* := *of Caml: if the value of* t *is a
reference* r *and the value of* u *is* v, *then the execution of the statement* *t =
u; *associates the value* v *to the reference* ι *in memory.*

Exercise 2.13

Show that the execution of the statement x = u; *has the same effect as
executing the statement* *&x = u. *What can we conclude?*

These constructs allow you to write a function swap *that takes as arguments two references and exchanges the values associated with these references
in memory.*

```
void swap (int* const x, int* const y) {
 int z;
 z = *x;
 *x = *y;
 *y = z;}
```

To exchange the values of the variables a *and* b, *you can now apply this function to the references* &a *and* &b.

```
int main () {
 a = 4;
 b = 7;
 swap(&a,&b);
 printf("%d\n",a);
 printf("%d\n",b);
 return 0;}
```

When we execute the statement swap(&a,&b); *in the environment* e = [a = r_1, b = r_2] *and the memory state* m = [r_1 = 4, r_2 = 7], *we create the environment* e = [a = r_1, b = r_2, x = r_1, y = r_2] *and the memory state* m = [r_1 = 4, r_2 = 7].

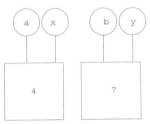

And, the function swap *exchanges the contents of the references* r_1 *and* r_2 *and after the execution of the function, the contents of the references associated with the variables* a *and* b *have been exchanged.*

In this example, take note of the syntax of the declaration of the argument x, int* const x, *which prevents the assignment* x = t; *but allows the assignment* *x = t;. *The declaration* const int* x, *in contrast allows the assignment* x = t; *but prevents the assignment* *x = t;. *The declaration* const int* const x *prevents both types of assignment.*

Exercise 2.14

What is the output of the following program?

```
void swap (int* x, int* y) {
 int z;
 z = *x;
```

```
  *x = *y;
  *y = z;}

int main () {
  a = 4;
  b = 7;
  swap(&a,&b);
  printf("%d\n",a);
  printf("%d\n",b);
  return 0;}
```

Draw the state in which the body of the function is executed.

Exercise 2.15

What does the following function do?

```
void swap1 (int* x, int* y) {
  int* z;
  z = x;
  x = y;
  y = z;}
```

Exercise 2.16

Give the definition of the Θ function for expressions of the form *t *and* &x, *and the definition for the* Σ *function for statements of the form* *t = u;.

Exercise 2.17

The goal of this exercise is to demonstrate that, in C, you may look for a reference that does not exist.

1. *In the following Caml program, what is the state in which the statement* print_int !(!u) *is executed?*

   ```
   let f p = let n = ref p in let x = ref n in !x
   in let u = ref (f 5)
   in print_int !(!u)
   ```

   Answer the same question for the following program.

   ```
   let f p = let n = ref p in let x = ref n in !x
   in let u = ref (f 5)
   in let v = ref (f 10)
   in print_int !(!u)
   ```

2. *Given the following C program*

```
int* f (const int p) {
 int n = p;
 int* x = &n;
 return x;}

int main () {
 int* u = f(5);
 printf("%d\n",*u);
 return 0;}
```

In what state is the statement `printf("%d\n",*u);` *executed?*

Hint: remember that in C, in contrast to Caml, we remove from memory the reference associated with a variable when that variable is removed from the environment.

3. *In C, when we use a reference that is not declared in memory, it does not produce an error, and the result will be unpredictable. Try compiling and running the following C program.*

```
int* f (const int p) {
 int n = p;
 int* x = &n;
 return x;}

int main () {
 int* u = f(5);
 int* v = f(10);
 printf("%d\n",*u);
 return 0;}
```

2.4.4 Java

In Java, passing by reference is not a primitive construct, but it can be simulated by using a different mechanism called *wrapper types*. We will explain this later, as it uses language constructs that have yet to be introduced.

Recursion

3.1 Calling a Function from Inside the Body of that Function

In the previous chapter, to define the Σ function for a statement of the form `f(t₁,...,tₙ);`, we have used the definition of the Σ function for the statement `p`, that is the body of the function `f`. Was this definition correct, or could it be circular?

This definition is clearly correct when the statement `p` does not contain within itself calls to another function. That is to say, when the main program — the `main` function — only calls functions that do not call functions themselves.

This definition is also correct when the program contains `k` function definitions f_1, ..., f_k such that the body of the function f_i contains only calls of functions defined before, that is to say functions f_j for $j < i$. Some languages, like Fortran, only allow the calling of a function `f` in the body of a function `g` if `f` is defined before `g`. In this case, the definition of the Σ function is by induction on three values: the number of the function, the number of nested `while` loops, and the size of the statement. Note that such an ordering of functions always exists if these functions are introduced from the main program by isolating parts of the program one after another: we isolate one part p_k of the main program, and then one part p_{k-1} of the main program or of the function p_k, ...

However, most programming languages allow functions to be written that call themselves, or that call functions that call other functions that eventually

G. Dowek, *Principles of Programming Languages*,
Undergraduate Topics in Computer Science, DOI 10.1007/978-1-84882-032-6_3,
© Springer-Verlag London Limited 2009

call the initial function.

This possibility is present in our definition of the Σ function for Java, since the global environment G is global for the whole program: all functions in the program can be called from within other functions. So, nothing prevents you from calling a function f in the body of a function g, whether function f is defined before g, after g, or if f and g are the same function.

We call *recursive function definitions* to be definitions of functions that call themselves, or that call functions that call other functions, that eventually call the initial function again. For recursive definitions, the definition of the Σ function from the previous chapter, can be circular. For example, if f is the function defined as follows

```
static void f (final int x) {f(x);}
```

then the definition of Σ(f(x);,e,m,G) uses the value of Σ(f(x);,e,m,G), which is circular.

We must therefore find another method of defining the Σ function.

3.2 Recursive Definitions

3.2.1 Recursive Definitions and Circular Definitions

A more interesting example of recursive definition is that of the factorial function

```
static int fact (final int x) {
 if (x == 0) return 1;
 return x * fact(x - 1);}
```

To compute the factorial of the number 3, we must compute the factorial of 2, which requires that we compute the factorial of 1, that requires the computation of the factorial of 0. This value is 1. The factorial of 1 is then found by multiplying 1 by this value, which gives 1. The factorial of 2 is found by multiplying 2 by this value, which gives 2. And the factorial of 3 is found by multiplying 3 by this value, which gives 6.

We sometimes say that a recursive definition is a definition that uses the object which it is defining. This idea is absurd: circular definitions are just as invalid in programming as they are elsewhere. If it were possible to use a function inside its own definition, the factorial function could be defined very simply

```
static int f (final int x) {return f(x);}
```

and the definition of the function that multiplies its argument by 4 or that squares it would be identical.

3.2.2 Recursive Definitions and Definitions by Induction

Another way to try to understand the definition of the function `fact` is to see it as a definition by induction of the sequence $u_n = n!$: $u_0 = 1$, $u_{n+1} = (n + 1) * u_n$. Although this works for this function, that does not mean it will work in general, for example for the function

```
static int f (final int n) {
 if (n <= 1) return 1;
 if (n % 2 == 0) return (1 + f(n / 2));
 return 2 * f(n + 1);}
```

Indeed, the computation of the value of this function at 11 requires the computation of its value at 12, which requires the computation of its value at 6, which requires the computation of its value at 3, which requires the computation of its value at 4, which requires the computation of its value at 2, which requires the computation of its value at 1. So, the computation of the value of the function f at n does not require only the computation of its value at n - 1, nor does it requires only the computation of its value at numbers smaller than n, but also that of its value at numbers larger than n. However, this definition is correct, and for any integer n, the computation of the value of f at n gives a result.

The function below presents a more interesting example

```
static int ack (final int x, final int y) {
 if (x == 0) return 2 * y;
 if (y == 0) return 1;
 return ack(x - 1,ack(x,y - 1));}
```

which always gives a result after a finite number of calls, but, as Wilhelm Ackermann proved in a theorem in 1928, cannot be defined using nested definitions by induction.

3.2.3 Recursive Definitions and Infinite Programs

When we have a recursive function definition, for example the definition of the factorial, it is possible to transform this definition into another, non-recursive one, by replacing the calls of the function `fact` in the body of the function `fact` by calls to another function `fact1`, identical to `fact`, but defined before it

```
static int fact1 (final int x) {
  if (x == 0) return 1;
  return x * fact1(x - 1);}
```

```
static int fact (final int x) {
  if (x == 0) return 1;
  return x * fact1(x - 1);}
```

The definition of the function `fact` is no longer recursive, but that of function `fact1` is. We can, as well, replace the calls to function `fact1` in the body of function `fact1` by calls to a function `fact2`, and so on. We can succeed, in theory, in creating a non-recursive program, but it will be infinitely long. Recursive definitions are, like the `while` loop, a means of expressing infinite programs and, like the `while` loop, recursive definitions introduce the possibility of non-termination.

Like in the case of `while` loops, we can introduce an imaginary expression, `giveup`, and approach this infinite program with finite approximations. We do this by replacing the nth copy of the function `fact` with the function `giveup` and remove the subsequent functions that are no longer used.

Calculating the value of the nth approximation of program p consists of trying to compute the value of program p by doing a maximum of n nested recursive calls. If at the end of these n calls, the computation is not complete, it is given up.

It isn't too difficult to prove that for any state `e, m`, either the sequence $\Sigma(p_n,e,m,G)$ is never defined or it is defined beyond a certain point, and in this case, it is constant over its domain. Remember that, in the second case, the limit of the sequence is the value that it takes over its domain and that the sequence has no limit if it is not defined.

We can now define the Σ function for (p,e,m,G)

$$\Sigma(p,e,m,G) = \lim_n \Sigma(p_n,e,m,G).$$

To generalise this idea to multiple mutually recursive functions, we will abandon the idea of copying out the recursive function calls, and instead introduce a parameter for the number of nested function calls. We define the family of functions Σ_k such that $\Sigma_k(p,e,m,G)$ is the result of executing the statement p, if the execution of this statement needs at most k nested function calls. If at the end of k nested calls, the computation is not complete, then the Σ_k function is not defined over (p,e,m,G).

The definition of the Σ_k functions is similar to the definition of the Σ function, except in the case of function calls. To define $\Sigma_k(f(t_1,\ldots,t_n);,e,m,G)$, we start by defining $(v_1,m_1) = \Theta_k(t_1,e,m,G)$, $(v_2,m_2) = \Theta_k(t_2,e,m_1,G)$, ..., $(v_n,m_n) = \Theta_k(t_n,e,m_{n-1},G)$, then e'' and m'' as we have done in the previous chapter. Next, instead of considering the object $\Sigma_k(p,e'',m'',G)$ we consider the object $\Sigma_{k-1}(p,e'',m'',G)$. A notable exception occurs in the case where k = 0, and in this case, the Σ_0 function is not defined for this expression.

Once the family of Σ_k functions is defined, we define the Σ function

$$\Sigma(\texttt{p,e,m,G}) = \texttt{lim}_k\ \Sigma_k(\texttt{p,e,m,G}).$$

3.2.4 Recursive Definitions and Fixed Point Equations

The recursive definition of the function called `fact`

```
static int fact (final int x) {
 if (x == 0) return 1;
 return x * fact(x - 1);}
```

cannot be seen as a regular definition, where the name `fact` is associated with an object. We can instead consider it as an equation where the variable is the function `fact`. Indeed, the function `fact` is the unique function f that maps natural numbers to natural numbers that satisfies the equation

$$\texttt{f = (x} \mapsto \texttt{if (x == 0) then 1 else x * f(x - 1)).}$$

This equation has the form `f = G(f)`, so it is a fixed point equation.

Some fixed point equations, for example, the equation

$$\texttt{f = (x} \mapsto \texttt{1 + f(x))}$$

that corresponds to the recursive definition

```
static int loop (final int x) {
 return 1 + loop(x);}
```

do not have any solutions when dealing with total functions that map integers to integers.

But, we have seen that recursively defined functions can be created that do not terminate. It is then among the partial functions that map integers to integers that we must find solutions. And, in this set, the fixed point equation

$$\texttt{f = (x} \mapsto \texttt{1 + f(x))}$$

has one solution that is the function with an empty domain.

We can prove that, in general, any fixed point equation always has at least one solution for the set of partial functions that map integers to integers. These various functions can be ordered by inclusion of their graphs, and we can prove that among these functions, one will be the smallest.

There is therefore an alternative method of defining the Σ function. However, this alternative definition is equivalent to the definition of Section 3.2.3, because this fixed point theorem produces a solution as the limit of a sequence of functions.

Exercise 3.1

What are all the solutions of the following equation?

$$f = (x \mapsto f(x))$$

What is the least solution?

Let `loop` be the function defined below

```
static int loop (final int x) {
 return loop(x);}
```

What is the value of the expression `loop(4)`?

Exercise 3.2

What are all the solutions of the following equation?

$$f = (x \mapsto 2 * f(x))$$

What is the least solution?

Let `loop` be the function defined below

```
static int loop (final int x) {
 return 2 * loop(x);}
```

What is the value of the expression `loop(4)`?

Exercise 3.3

In the set of partial functions that map integers to integers, what are all the solutions to the following equation?

$$f = (x \mapsto if (x == 0) then 1 else x * f(x - 1))$$

What is the least solution?

Imagine a data type that allows integers to be of any size. What does the call `fact(-1)` return?

In the set of partial functions from an interval to itself, what are all the solutions of this equation?

What does the call `fact(-100)` return if we define the function `fact` as follows?

```
static byte fact (final byte x) {
 if (x == 0) return 1;
 return (byte) (x * fact((byte) (x - 1)));}
```

Why? And what does the call `fact(-100)` return if we define the function `fact` as follows?

```
static double fact (final byte x) {
 if (x == 0) return 1.0;
 return x * fact((byte) (x - 1));}
```

Why?

3.3 Caml

In Caml, we execute the body of the function in the environment in which the function was declared, extended by the declaration of its arguments. Because of this fact, only functions declared before the function f *are accessible within the body of* f, *and the declaration*

```
let fact x = if x = 0 then 1 else x * fact(x - 1)
in print_int (fact 6)
```

is invalid.

   To be able to use the function `fact` *within its own definition, you must use a new construct* `let rec f x₁ ... xₙ = t in p`

```
let rec fact x = if x = 0 then 1 else x * fact(x - 1)
in print_int (fact 6)
```

and, at each function call, the definition of the function `fact` *is then added to the environment in which the body of the function is executed.*

   When two functions are mutually recursive, you cannot declare them as follows

```
let rec even x = if x = 0 then true else odd(x - 1)
in let rec odd x = if x = 0 then false else even(x - 1)
in print_bool(even 7)
```

because the environment in which the function even *is executed does not contain the function* odd, *so we have to use a special construct for mutually recursive functions* let rec f x$_1$ ... x$_n$ = t and g y$_1$ ... y$_p$ = u and ... *For example*

```
let rec even x = if x = 0 then true else odd (x - 1)
and odd x = if x = 0 then false else even (x - 1)
in print_bool (even 7)
```

3.4 C

In C, as in Caml, the body of the function is executed in the environment in which this function was declared, extended with the declaration of its arguments. Because of this, only functions declared before a function f *are accessible in the body of* f.

However, in order to allow for recursion, at each function call, the definition of the function f *is added to the environment in which the body of the function is executed. This is exactly what happens in Caml with* let rec, *so the declaration of a function in C is more like Caml's* let rec *than it is like* let. *Therefore, the following program*

```
int fact (const int x) {
 if (x == 0) return 1;
 return x * fact(x - 1);}

int main () {
 printf("%d\n",fact(6));
 return 0;}
```

is valid, and returns 720.

When the definitions of several functions, for example two functions f *and* g, *are mutually recursive, we must start by* prototyping *the function* g *to allow* g *to be called within the body of* f. *Prototyping a function defines its argument types and its return type, and you can then define the actual function later in the program.*

```
int odd (const int);

int even (const int x) {
 if (x == 0) return 1;
 return odd(x - 1);}
```

```
int odd (const int x) {
 if (x == 0) return 0;
 return even(x - 1);}

int main () {
 printf("%d\n",even(7));
 return 0;}
```

3.5 Programming Without Assignment

Comparing the factorial function written with a loop

```
static int fact (final int x) {
 int i;
 int r;

 r = 1;
 for (i = 1; i <= x; i = i + 1) {r = r * i;}
 return r;}
```

and recursively

```
static int fact (final int x) {
 if (x == 0) return 1;
 return x * fact(x - 1);}
```

we see that the first uses assignments: r = 1;, i = 1;, i = i + 1; and r = r * i;, while the second does not. It is therefore possible to program the factorial function without using assignments.

More generally, we can consider a sub-language of Java in which we remove assignment. In this case, all variables can be declared as constant and, in the definition of the Σ function, the memory state is always empty. Sequences and loops in this case become useless. We are left with a shell of Java composed of variable declarations, function calls, arithmetical and logical operations and tests. This sub-language is called the *functional core* of Java. We can also define the functional core of many programming languages.

Surprisingly, this functional core is just as powerful as Java as a whole. For each expression t of Java, we associate the partial function that maps the integer n to the value v such that (v,m') = Θ(t,[x = n],[],G), and for each statement p in Java we associate the partial function that maps the integer n to the value v such that (return,v,m) = Σ(p,[x = n],[],G). A partial function f that maps integers to integers is called *programmable* in Java if there exists an expression t or a statement p such that f is the function associated with t or with p.

We can show that the set of programmable functions in Java, in the imperative core of Java or in its functional core is identical: it is the set of computable functions — see Exercise 1.12.

This result is true only because we allow for recursive functions. Loops and recursion are therefore two essentially redundant constructs for producing infinite programs, and each time you want to construct an infinite program, you can choose to use either a loop or a recursive definition.

Exercise 3.4

Write the definition of the Σ function for the functional core of Java.

Exercise 3.5 (The Towers of Hanoi)

The towers of Hanoi is a game created by Édouard Lucas in 1883. It has seven disks of different sizes distributed among three columns. At the start, all the disks are on the left column, arranged from largest to smallest, with the largest disk on the bottom.

The only movement allowed is to move a single disk from the top of one column to the top of another column, with the condition that you can never place a bigger disk on top of a smaller one. We write n -> n' the movement of a disk from column n to column n'. The goal of the game is to move all of the disks from the left column to the right column.

Write a program that generates a solution to the game by outputting a list of movements.

Hint: A variant of the game has only six disks. If one can solve the game for six disks, how can one solve the game for seven disks?

Exercise 3.6 (The Koch Snowflake)

The Koch Snowflake, created in 1906 by Helge Von Koch, is an example of a non-differentiable continuous curve. It's also an example of a fractal set, that is to say a set whose Hausdorff dimension is not a whole number.

This curve is defined as the limit of the sequence of curves where the first curve is a segment

and where each element is obtained from the previous one, by dividing each segment in 3, and replacing the middle segment with an equilateral triangle with one side removed. The second iteration of the Koch snowflake is thus

the third

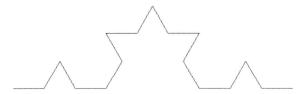

and the fourth

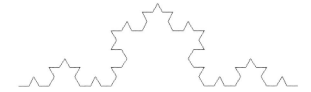

Write a program that draws the nth element of this sequence.

4
Records

In the programs that have been described in previous chapters, each variable contained an integer, a decimal number, a boolean, or a character.

These variables could not contain an object composed of several numbers, booleans or characters, such as a complex number made of two decimal numbers, a vector made of several coordinates, or a string made of several characters.

We will now introduce a new construct, *records*, that allow the construction of these composite objects.

4.1 Tuples with Named Fields

Mathematically, a tuple is a function whose domain is a set of the form {0, 1, ..., n - 1}. In programming languages, tuples are usually of *named fields*, that is, they are functions where the domain is not of the form {0, 1, ..., n - 1}, but an arbitrary finite set, whose elements are called *labels*. Such a tuple of named fields is called a *record*.

For example, if we are given a set of labels `latitude`, `longitude` and `altitude`, we can construct the record {latitude = 48.715, longitude = 2.208, altitude = 156.0}.

G. Dowek, *Principles of Programming Languages*,
Undergraduate Topics in Computer Science, DOI 10.1007/978-1-84882-032-6_4,
© Springer-Verlag London Limited 2009

4.1.1 The Definition of a Record Type

In Java, we define a new type of records by indicating the label and type of each of its fields. For example, the type `Point` is defined as

```
class Point {
 final double latitude;
 final double longitude;
 final double altitude;}
```

This definition is written before the introduction of the name of the program with the keyword `class`.

4.1.2 Allocation of a Record

Once this type is defined, you can declare a variable with the type `Point`.

```
Point x;
```

As with any variable declaration, this adds an ordered pair to the environment that associates a reference `r` to this variable, and an ordered pair to the memory that associates a value to the reference `r`. If we declare this variable without giving it a value, the value by default is a special value called `null`. We represent a state, in which the variable `x` is associated in the environment to a reference `r`, which is associated in the memory to the value `null` this way.

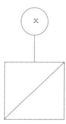

In Java, the reference `r` is never directly associated to a record in memory. The box `r` is always a small box that can only contain `null` or another reference.

To associate a record with the variable `x`, you start by creating a box large enough to contain three decimal numbers. This is done with a new construct: `new`

```
new Point()
```

The evaluation of the expression `new Point()` creates a new reference `r'` and associates this reference with a record, by default {`latitude = 0.0`, longitude = 0.0, altitude = 0.0}. The value of this expression is the reference r'.

In this diagram, the object on the right is only one box that can contain three decimal numbers, and not a collection of three boxes. Seen another way, there is only one reference r'.

A reference that was added to memory by the construct new is called a *cell*. The set of memory cells is called the *heap*. The operation that adds a new cell to the memory state, is called an *allocation*.

When you execute the statement

```
x = new Point();
```

you associate the reference r' to the reference r in memory. The environment is then [x = r] and the memory state [r = r', r' = {latitude = 0.0, longitude = 0.0, altitude = 0.0}].

In Java, as in Caml and C, references are values and it is possible for a reference to be associated to another reference. But unlike Caml and C, this can only be done using this construct for records.

It is possible to declare the variable x with an initial value. Instead of writing

```
Point x;
x = new Point();
```

you can write

```
Point x = new Point();
```

Like any variable, a variable of type Point can be mutable or constant. So, whereas the statement

```
Point x = new Point();
```

creates the environment [x = r] and the memory state [r = r', r' = {latitude = 0.0, longitude = 0.0, altitude = 0.0}], the statement

```
final Point x = new Point();
```

creates the environment [x = r'] and the memory state [r' = {latitude = 0.0, longitude = 0.0, altitude = 0.0}].

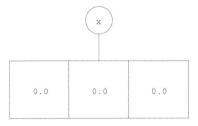

Although it is associated with a variable in the environment, the reference r' is a cell, since it was created with the statement new.

4.1.3 Accessing Fields

If the value of the expression t is a reference r' associated in memory with a record and l is a label, the value of the expression t.l is the field l of this record. So, the statement

```
System.out.println(x.longitude);
```

outputs 0.0.

In particular, when t is a mutable variable x, its value is m(e(x)) and so the value of the expression x.latitude is the field latitude of the record m(m(e(x))). In contrast, when t is a constant variable x, its value is e(x) and so the value of the expression x.latitude is the field latitude of the record m(e(x)).

4.1.4 Assignment of Fields

In the definition of a record, it is also possible that the fields are mutable

```
class Point {
 double latitude;
 double longitude;
 double altitude;}
```

In this case, when you execute the statement

```
Point x = new Point();
```

you might think you are creating the environment `[x = r]` and the memory state `[r = r', r' = {latitude =` r_1`, longitude =` r_2`, altitude =` r_3`},` r_1 `= 0.0,` r_2 `= 0.0,` r_3 `= 0.0]`.

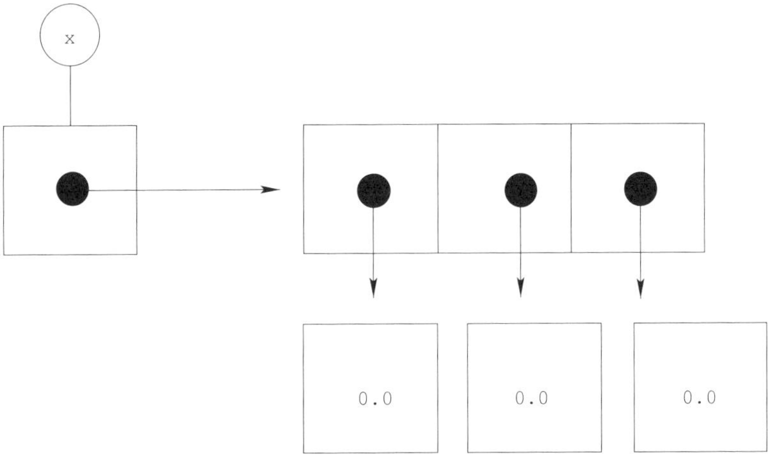

But, this is not the case: you have already introduced a reference `r'` by creating the cell and you can use this to make fields mutable without introducing extra references. Whether the fields are constant or mutable, you are constructing the environment `[x = r]` and the memory state `[r = r', r' = {latitude = 0.0, longitude = 0.0, altitude = 0.0}]`

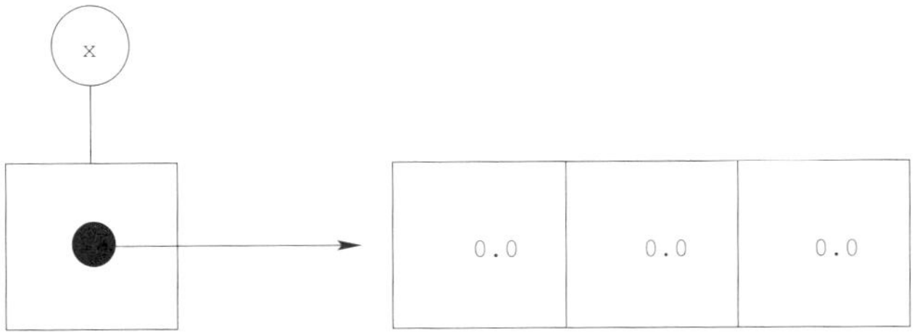

In this cell, you simply choose which fields are mutable and which are constant.

To assign to a record's mutable field, you use a new statement `t.l = u;`, where `l` is a label and `t` and `u` are expressions. If the value of expression `t` is a reference `r` associated in memory with a record that has a field `l`, then when you execute the statement `t.l = u;`, the field `l` of this record receives the value of expression `u`.

Thus, in executing the statements

```
x.latitude = 48.715;
```

```
x.longitude = 2.208;
x.altitude = 156.0;
```

you create the state

   The means of handling records in a programming language, like Java, is therefore composed of four constructs that allow you to

– define a type, `class` in Java,

– allocate a cell, `new` in Java,

– access a field, `t.l` in Java,

– assign to a field, `t.l = u;` in Java.

Understanding how records are handled in a new programming language requires you to understand the constructs that allow you to define a type, allocate a cell, access a field, and assign to a field.

4.1.5 Constructors

We have seen how to allocate a cell

```
x = new Point();
```

and assigning to its fields

```
x.latitude = 48.715;
x.longitude = 2.208;
x.altitude = 156.0;
```

It is possible to do all of this in a single statement

```
x = new Point(48.715,2.208,156.0);
```

But this requires an improvement to the definition of the `Point` type, by adding a *constructor*

```
class Point {
 double latitude;
 double longitude;
 double altitude;

 Point (final double x, final double y, final double z) {
  this.latitude = x; this.longitude = y; this.altitude = z;}}
```

A constructor definition resembles the declaration of a function: a constructor has arguments of a certain type, and a body that is executed at the moment it is called. But

− a constructor must always have the same name as the type it belongs to,

− in the definition of a constructor, you never define a return type,

− you never use the **return** statement in the body of a constructor,

− in the body of a constructor, you can assign to fields of the allocated record using the keyword **this** to refer to this record.

It is possible to define multiple constructors for the same type. Since these constructors must have the same name, they are overloaded and must be distinguished by the number or type of their arguments. For example, it is possible to add a constructor to the type **Point** with two arguments that constructs a point of altitude 0.

Finally, when no constructor is defined, there is a default constructor with no arguments, which we have used above in the expression **new Point()**. You cannot use the default constructor once one has been defined in your program.

Finally, when declaring a type, it is also possible to define default values for each field

```
class Point {
 double latitude = 90.0;
 double longitude = 0.0;
 double altitude = 0.0;}
```

In this case, if a constructor does not assign to a field of the object **this**, the default value used is not 0.0, but the value given in that definition.

4.1.6 The Semantics of Records

To extend the Σ function to cover records, it is necessary to add a fifth argument that is the list of constructed types, each type being associated to an ordered pair composed of a list of its fields and a list of its constructors.

Exercise 4.1

Define the Σ function for the four operations: type definition, cell allocation, accessing to a field, assigning to a field.

4.2 Sharing

4.2.1 Sharing

Suppose that x and y are two variables of type Point, associated with two references r_1 and r_2 in the environment. In addition, suppose that, in memory, r_1 is associated with a reference r_3, which itself is associated with a record {latitude = 48.715, longitude = 2.208, altitude = 156.0} and r_2 with a reference r_4, which itself is associated with the record {latitude = 90.0, longitude = 0.0, altitude = 0.0}. So, e = [x = r_1, y = r_2], m = [r_1 = r_3, r_2 = r_4, r_3 = {latitude = 48.715, longitude = 2.208, altitude = 156.0}, r_4 = {latitude = 90.0, longitude = 0.0, altitude = 0.0}].

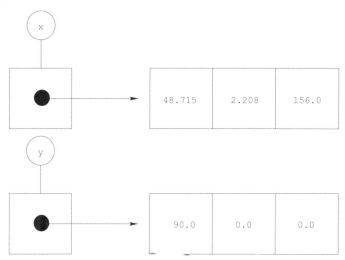

When the statement y = x; is executed, the value of x is computed, which is the reference r_3 and we associate this value with the reference r_2. The memory state becomes [r_1 = r_3, r_2 = r_3, r_3 = {latitude = 48.715, longitude = 2.208, altitude = 156.0}, r_4 = {latitude = 90.0, longitude = 0.0, altitude = 0.0}].

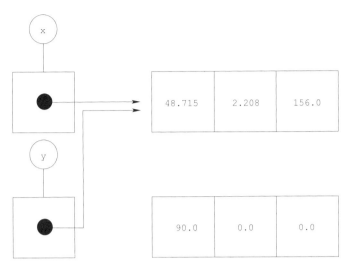

In contrast, if the statements y.latitude = x.latitude; y.longitude = x.longitude; y.altitude = x.altitude; are executed, the resultant memory state is [r_1 = r_3, r_2 = r_4, r_3 = {latitude = 48.715, longitude = 2.208, altitude = 156.0}, r_4 = {latitude = 48.715, longitude = 2.208, altitude = 156.0}].

If you then assign to the field latitude of the record x: x.latitude = 23.45; and then output the field latitude of y, you get 23.45 in the first case, and 48.715 in the second. We say, in the first case, that the variables x and y *share* the cell r_3. All changes of the cell associated with x automatically change the cell associated with y, and vice versa.

4.2.2 Equality

If a and b are two expressions of type Point, their value is a reference and the expression a == b evaluates to true only when these two references are identical. That is to say when a and b share the same cell. We call this type of equality *physical*. So, the program

```
Point a = new Point(48.715,2.208,156.0);
Point b = new Point(48.715,2.208,156.0);
if (a == b) System.out.println("equal");
else System.out.println("different");
```

outputs different.

It is also possible to write a function that tests the *structural* equality of two records, which checks the equality of their fields

```
static boolean equal (final Point x, final Point y) {
  return (x.latitude == y.latitude)
      && (x.longitude == y.longitude)
      && (x.altitude == y.altitude);}
```

and the statement

```
if (equal(a,b)) System.out.println("equal");
else System.out.println("different");
```

outputs equal.

4.2.3 Wrapper Types

A *wrapper* is a type of record with one lone field. An example is the type Integer

```
class Integer {
  int c;

  Integer (int x) {
    this.c = x;}}
```

At first glance, the Integer type and the int type may seem redundant, because the record {c = 4} is not very different from the integer 4. And it is true that the program

```
Integer x = new Integer(4);
Integer y = new Integer(x.c);
```

```
x.c = 5;
System.out.println(y.c);
```

can be rewritten as

```
int x = 4;
int y = x;
x = 5;
System.out.println(y);
```

which produces the same result: both output the number 4.

However, if you replace the statement `Integer y = new Integer(x.c);` with `Integer y = x;` instead of obtaining the state

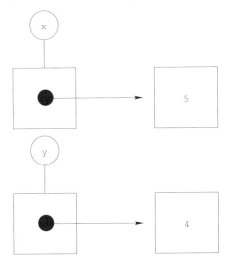

you obtain the state

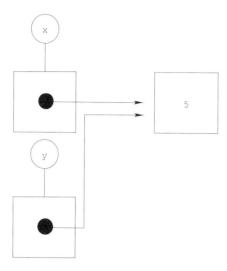

and the program outputs 5, instead of 4.

More generally, instead of having a state in which a variable x is associated with a reference r associated with a value, for example, 4

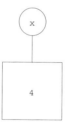

wrapper types allows you to have a state in which a variable x is associated with a reference r, associated with a reference r', which is itself associated with the value 4.

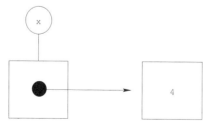

This type of indirection allows several variables to share a single value. In Caml and in C, this allows you to write functions with arguments that are passed by reference, like the function swap that swaps the contents of its arguments, and more generally, functions that modify their arguments.

In Java, it is not possible to write a function that swaps the contents of two arguments of type `int`. However, it is possible with arguments of type `Integer`.

```
static void swap (Integer x, Integer y) {
  int z = x.c;
  x.c = y.c;
  y.c = z;}
```

and the program

```
public static void main (String [] args) {
  a = new Integer(4);
  b = new Integer(7);
  swap(a,b);
  System.out.println(a.c + "   " + b.c);}
```

outputs 7 and 4.

Wrapper types allow you to simulate passing arguments by reference in Java.

Indeed, when you call the function `swap`, you create the state

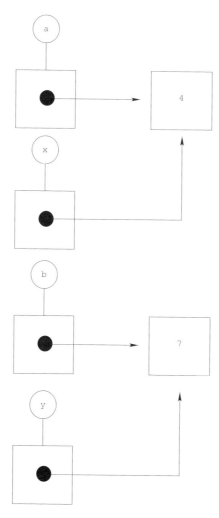

and swapping the contents of x and y will also swap those of a and b.

If variables a, b, x and y are constant and of the type Integer, then the state created is as follows

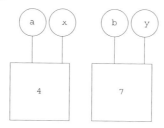

and swapping the contents of x and y swaps those of a and b.

Exercise 4.2

In which state is the body of the function `swap` executed if `a` and `b` are constant, but `x` and `y` are mutable? And if `a` and `b` are mutable, but `x` and `y` are constant?

Exercise 4.3

What does the following program output, if you replace the function `swap` with the function `swap1` defined below?

```
static void swap1 (Integer x, Integer y) {
  Integer z = x;
  x = y;
  y = z;}
```

4.3 Caml

We will now see constructs in Caml that allow you to define a type, allocate a cell, read a field, and assign to a field.

4.3.1 Definition of a Record Type

In Caml, as in Java, you define a record type by defining the type and label of each of its fields.

```
type point = {
 latitude : float;
 longitude : float;
 altitude : float;}
```

4.3.2 Creating a Record

You create a value to assign to each of its fields {latitude = 90.0; longitude = 0.0; altitude = 0.0;}. *There is no* new *keyword, and the pair of braces indicates that you want to allocate a cell.*

The declaration let x = ref {latitude = 90.0; longitude = 0.0; altitude = 0.0;} *creates the state*

And, with a constant variable, the declaration let x = {latitude = 90.0; longitude = 0.0; altitude = 0.0;} *creates the state*

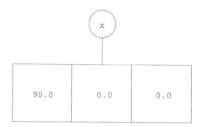

A variable x *of type* point ref *is always associated with a reference, which itself is associated with a record in memory. There is no* null *value in Caml.*

4.3.3 Accessing Fields

If the value of expression t *is a reference* r' *associated in memory with a record, the value of expression* t.l *is the field* l *of this record.*

In particular, when t *is of the form* !x *where* x *is a mutable variable, its value is* m(e(x)) *and so the value of expression* (!x).latitude *is the field* latitude *of the record* m(m(e(x))), *like the value of the expression* x.latitude *in Java. And when* t *is a constant variable* x, *its value is* e(x) *and so the value of the expression* x.latitude *is the field* latitude *of the record* m(e(x)) *as in Java.*

4.3.4 Assigning to Fields

In Caml, all fields are constant by default, and you must indicate that they should be mutable with the keyword mutable.

```
type int_wrap = {mutable c : int}
```

Mutable field assignment is written as x.c <- 4.
    The function

```
let swap x y = let z = x.c in (x.c <- y.c; y.c <- z)
```

swaps the contents of two variables of type int_wrap. *When you execute the statement* swap a b *in the state composed of the environment* [a = r, b = r'] *and the memory state* [r = 4, r' = 7]

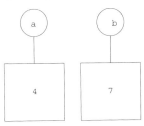

the values associated with variables x *and* y *are the references* r *and* r' *and not the integers* 4 *and* 7

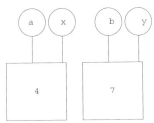

and so swapping the contents of x *and* y *swaps the contents of* a *and* b.

You can avoid using the construct ref *by using a constant variable of a wrapper type, like in Java. In fact, the type* int ref *of Caml is not primitive, but is an abbreviation for a wrapper type like this one.*

Exercise 4.4

What is the state created by the following declarations?

```
type point = {
 mutable latitude : float;
 mutable longitude : float;
 mutable altitude : float;}

let x = {latitude = 48.715;
         longitude = 2.208;
         altitude = 156.0;}
```

and by the following declarations?

```
type point = {
```

```
  latitude : float ref;
  longitude : float ref;
  altitude : float ref;}

let x = {latitude = ref 48.715;
         longitude = ref 2.208;
         altitude = ref 156.0;}
```

Draw both of these states.

4.4 C

4.4.1 Definition of a Record Type

In C, we define a record type, called a structure, *by defining the label and type of each of its fields*

```
struct Point {
 double latitude;
 double longitude;
 double altitude;};
```

4.4.2 Creating a Record

Like in Java, a variable can be declared of type Point

```
struct Point x;
```

with the difference that the keyword struct *must always be written before the type name. It is also possible to avoid giving the type a name, and to apply the type directly to the variable* x *as follows*

```
struct {double latitude; double longitude; double altitude;} x;
```

It is also possible to give an initial value while declaring the variable

```
struct Point x = {90.0,0.0,0.0};
```

In contrast with Java, a single declaration creates a record with three fields. There is therefore no equivalent to the **new** construct from Java. In C, creating records does not allocate cells.

A variable of type `Point` can never have the value `null`. It directly associates, in the environment, the variable `x` with a reference `r` and, in memory, the
reference `r` to the record {latitude = 90.0, longitude = 0.0, altitude =
0.0}. Therefore, there is one less level of indirection than is found in Java.

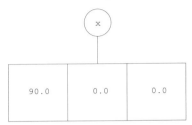

4.4.3 Accessing Fields

You can then access fields of the record

```
printf("%f\n",x.latitude);
```

If the value of expression `t` is a record, the value of expression `t.l` is the field
`l` of this record. Specifically, when `t` is a variable `x`, its value is `m(e(x))` and
so the value of expression `x.latitude` is the field `latitude` of record `m(e(x))`
and not `m(m(e(x)))` like in Java.

4.4.4 Assigning to Fields

You can then assign to a record's field

```
x.latitude = 48.715;
x.longitude = 2.208;
x.altitude = 156.0;
```

When you define a function

```
void tropic (struct Point y) {
 y.latitude = 23.45;}
```

and call it with the statement

```
tropic(x);
```

the value of `x` is not a reference associated with a record in memory as it is
in Java and Caml, but the record itself and is recopied to the variable `y` at the
moment of the function call.

Thus, the program

```
int main () {
 struct Point x = {90.0,0.0,0.0};
 x.latitude = 48.715;
 x.longitude = 2.208;
 x.altitude = 156.0;
 tropic(x);
 printf("%f\n",x.latitude);
 return 0;}
```

outputs 48.715 *and not* 23.45.

The use of a structure does not allow you to write functions with argument passing by reference. For a function to take a record as an argument and modify its fields, you must use the construct &*, as in the case of an argument of a scalar type*

```
void tropic (struct Point* y) {
 (*y).latitude = 23.45;}
```

```
tropic(&x);
```

The statement

```
struct Point x = {90.0,0.0,0.0};
struct Point* y = &x;
```

creates the state

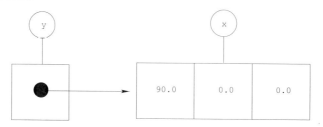

Records in Java correspond to references to records in C. While in Java you would write t.l, *in C you would write* (*t).l.

Exercise 4.5

What does the following program output?

```
struct Integer {
 int c;};

void swap (struct Integer x, struct Integer y) {
 int z = x.c;
 x.c = y.c;
 y.c = z;}

int main () {
 struct Integer a = {4};
 struct Integer b = {7};
 swap(a,b);
 printf("%d\n",a.c);
 return 0;}
```

4.5 Arrays

Programming languages allow you to also create tuples where the fields are not named, but are identified by number. We call them *arrays*.

The fields of an array, in contrast to those of a record, are all of the same type. The number of fields of an array is determined during the allocation of the array, and not during the declaration of its type, as is the case with records. This allows you to compute, during the execution of a program, an integer n and to allocate an array of size n. It is also possible to compute, during execution of a program, an integer k and to access the kth field of an array, or to assign to it.

However, once an array is allocated, it is not possible to change its size. The only way to accomplish this is to allocate a new array of a different size and to copy the fields of the old one to the new one.

4.5.1 Array Types

In Java, an array with elements of type T is of type T [].

4.5.2 Allocation of an Array

You can, for example, give the type int [] to a variable.

```
int [] t;
```

   As with any variable declaration, this adds an ordered pair to the environment that associates a reference r to the variable t and an ordered pair to the memory that associates a value with the reference r. If you declare this variable without giving it a value, the value by default is null. In Java, the reference r is never directly associated with an array of values in memory. The box r can only contain null or another reference.

   To associate an array with the variable t, you start by creating a box large enough to contain several integers. This is done with the statement new

```
new int [10]
```

Evaluation of the expression new int [u], where u is an expression whose value is an integer n, creates a new reference r' and associates this reference with a n-tuple containing the default values: 0 in this case. The fields are numbered from 0 to n - 1.

   The statement

```
t = new int [10];
```

associates the reference r' with the reference r in memory. The environment is then [t = r] and the memory state is [r = r', r' = [0,0,0,0,0,0,0,0,0, 0]]. It is possible to declare a variable t with an initial value. Instead of writing

```
int [] t;
t = new int [10];
```

you can write

```
int [] t = new int [10];
```

4.5.3 Accessing and Assigning to Fields

If the value of the expression t is a reference associated in memory to an array and the value of expression u is an integer k, the value of expression t[u] is the value contained in the kth field of the array. Thus, the statement

```
System.out.println(t[5]);
```

outputs 0.

   To assign to the kth field of an array, we use a new statement t[u] = v where t is an expression whose value is a reference associated in memory with an array, `u` is an expression whose value is an integer `k` and `v` an expression of the same type as the elements in the array. When you execute this statement, the kth field of the array receives the value of expression `v`.

Thus, the program

```
int [] t = new int [10];
int k = 5;
t[k] = 4;
System.out.println(t[k]);
```

outputs 4.

Exercise 4.6

We can represent natural numbers of up to 110 digits by using an array of digits, each digit being of type `int`.

1. Define addition, subtraction, multiplication, and euclidean division for these numbers.

2. Knowing that
$$\tan(2\ x) = \frac{2\tan(x)}{1 - \tan^2(x)}$$
and
$$\tan(x - \frac{\pi}{4}) = \frac{\tan(x) - 1}{\tan(x) + 1}$$
we show that
$$\tan(4\arctan(\frac{1}{5}) - \frac{\pi}{4}) = \frac{1}{239}.$$
As $\frac{1}{5} \leq \sqrt{2} - 1$, we have $\arctan(\frac{1}{5}) \leq \arctan(\sqrt{2} - 1) = \frac{\pi}{8}$ and so
$$-\frac{\pi}{2} < 4\arctan(\frac{1}{5}) - \frac{\pi}{4} < \frac{\pi}{2}$$
thus
$$4\arctan(\frac{1}{5}) - \frac{\pi}{4} = \arctan(\frac{1}{239})$$
that is to say
$$\pi = 16\arctan(\frac{1}{5}) - 4\arctan(\frac{1}{239})$$
$$\pi = \sum_{i=0}^{\infty} \frac{16(-1)^i}{5^{2i+1}(2i + 1)} - \sum_{i=0}^{\infty} \frac{4(-1)^i}{239^{2i+1}(2i + 1)}.$$

This series, which converges much more rapidly than $\pi = 4\arctan(1)$ because the numbers $\frac{1}{5}$ and $\frac{1}{239}$ are smaller than 1, was used in 1706 by John Machin to compute the first hundred decimal places of π.

Let

$$\hat{\pi} = 10^{-104} \left(\sum_{i=0}^{71} (-1)^i \left\lfloor \frac{10^{104} 16}{5^{2i+1}(2i+1)} \right\rfloor - \sum_{i=0}^{20} (-1)^i \left\lfloor \frac{10^{104} 4}{239^{2i+1}(2i+1)} \right\rfloor \right)$$

where $\lfloor x \rfloor$ is the floor of x. Show that

$$|\pi - \hat{\pi}| \leq 10^{-101}.$$

Show that, if the 101st decimal place of $\hat{\pi}$ is neither a 0 or 9, then the first hundred decimal places of π and $\hat{\pi}$ are the same.

3. Write a Java program that computes $\hat{\pi}$. What is its 101st decimal place? What are the first 100 decimal places of π?

4.5.4 Arrays of Arrays

In order to represent tuples indexed with ordered pairs or ordered triplets of integers, such as matrices, one possibility is to create an array whose elements are themselves arrays. The element at index (i,j) of array t is written t[i][j]. Such an array has the type T [][].

Allocation of such an array is done with a single operation

```
int [][] t = new int [20][20];
```

Exercise 4.7

The *game of life* is a game invented by John Conway in 1970. On a grid, you lay out creatures randomly. The population of these creatures evolves from one state to the next based on the following rules.

– A creature survives if it has 2 or 3 neighbours in the 8 adjacent cells, and it dies due to isolation or overpopulation otherwise.

– A creature is born in an empty cell if it has exactly 3 neighbours in the 8 adjacent cells, and no creature is born in that cell otherwise.

For example, starting with the initial state

the population evolves as follows

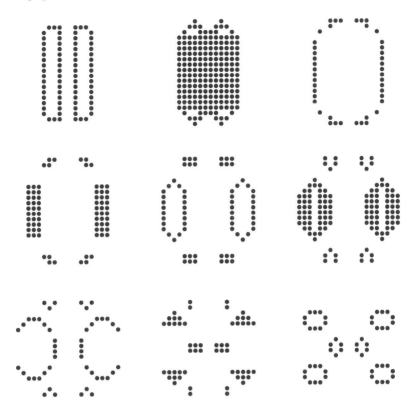

Write a program that implements the game of life, so you can observe the development of a population of creatures.

4.5.5 Arrays in Caml

In Caml, an array with elements of type T *is of the type* T array. *You allocate an array with the expression* Array.make u v *where* u *is an expression whose value is an integer* n *and* v *is an expression of type* T. *The array that is created has size* n *and each field receives the value of expression* v *as its initial value.*

If the value of expression t *is a reference associated in memory with an array and the value of expression* u *is an integer* k, *the value of the expression* Array.get t u *is the value contained in the* k[th] *field of this array.*

To assign to the kth *field of an array, you use the new statement* Array.set t u v *where* t *is an expression whose value is a reference associated in memory with an array,* u *and an expression whose value is an integer* k, *and* v *is an* *expression of the same type as the elements of the array. When you execute this statement, the kth field of the array receives the value of expression v.*

So, the program

```
let t = Array.make 10 0
in let k = 5
in Array.set t k 4; print_int (Array.get t k)
```

outputs 4.

4.5.6 Arrays in C

In C, arrays, like records, are not allocated. Because of this fact, the size of an array cannot be determined at the moment of its allocation, and is part of its type.

An array of size n whose elements are of type T are of type $T[n]$. You declare a variable t of type $T[n]$ as follows

```
T t [n];
```

For example

```
int t [10];
```

The size of an array is not necessarily constant, but can be any integer expression. The array created has size n and each field receives an unspecified initial value.

In C, as in Java and Caml, the value of the variable t is a reference associated in memory with an array. The arrays are therefore somewhat different from records. If the value of expression t is a reference associated in memory with an array and the value of expression u is an integer k, the value of expression $t[u]$ is the value contained in the kth field of this array. To assign to the kth field of an array, you use a new statement $t[u] = v$ where t is an expression whose value is a reference associated in memory with an array, u is an expression whose value is an integer k and v is an expression of the same type as the elements in the array. When you execute this statement, the kth field of the array receives the value of expression v. So, the program

```
int t [10];
int k = 5;
t[k] = 4;
printf("%d\n",t[k]);
```

outputs 4.

5
Dynamic Data Types

Records allow you to construct data types composed of several numbers or characters. But all the values of a particular type of record must have the same number of fields. It is not possible to define a record without knowing ahead of time how many fields it will contain, like a polynomial, a string of characters, a dictionary, or an address book.

You can represent these types of objects using arrays, but the size of an array is determined during its allocation. Because of this, when you represent, for example, large integers in an array, like in Exercise 4.6, you have to choose the number of digits ahead of time.

In this chapter, we will see how to represent data where the size is restricted only by the size of the computer's memory, which is always finite. We call *dynamic data* such composite data whose size is not known ahead of time, and if the data is mutable, can change size during the execution of the program.

5.1 Recursive Records

5.1.1 Lists

In the previous chapter, we created a record type whose fields were of the scalar type `double`. It is also possible to define a record type `T` whose fields are themselves records, in particular the type `T` itself. For example, a triplet

G. Dowek, *Principles of Programming Languages*,
Undergraduate Topics in Computer Science, DOI 10.1007/978-1-84882-032-6_5,
© Springer-Verlag London Limited 2009

of integers (a,b,c) can be defined as the pair (a,(b,c)), and more generally a non-empty *list* of integers can be defined as an ordered pair composed of an integer, the *head* of the list, and a shorter list, the *tail* of the list. Thus, the type List is defined as follows

```
class List {
 int hd;
 List tl;}
```

The head of the list 1, 2, 3, 4, for example, is the integer 1. The tail of this list is the list 2, 3, 4 — and not the integer 4.

5.1.2 The null Value

This definition is not complete, because if List is the type of lists, the cartesian product int × List contains only non-empty lists. The type List is therefore not the cartesian product int × List, but the disjoint union {empty} ⊎ (int × List).

However, since a value of the type List is either null or a reference associated in memory with a record, the type List that we have defined is equal to {null} ⊎ (int × List), so that the empty list and the value null get identified.

5.1.3 An Example

Observe what happens when you execute the following program

```
List l;
l = new List();
l.hd = 4;
l.tl = new List();
l.tl.hd = 5;
l.tl.tl = null;
```

The declaration List l; associates the variable l with a reference r in the environment, and associates the reference r with the default value null in memory

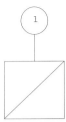

then the statement `l = new List();` allocates a cell `r'`, fills this cell with the default values `0` and `null`, and assigns the reference `r'` to the variable `l`

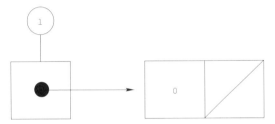

The statement `l.hd = 4;` assigns the value 4 to the field `hd` of the cell

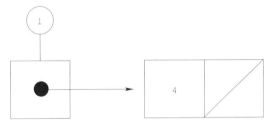

The statement `l.tl = new List();` allocates a new cell

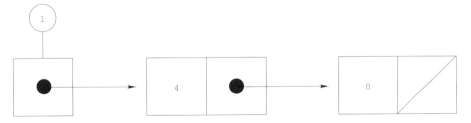

Then, the last two statements assign to the fields of this cell

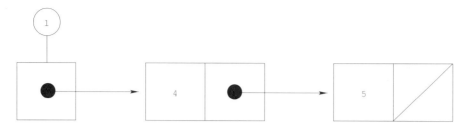

You can also define a constructor in the declaration of type `List`

```
List (final int x, final List y) {this.hd = x; this.tl = y;}
```

and write this program more concisely

```
List l = new List(4,new List(5,null));
```

Thus, it seems that this recursive definition defines a type whose elements are lists of integers.

Exercise 5.1

Write a function that computes the sum of the elements of a list of integers.

5.1.4 Recursive Definitions and Fixed Point Equations

In the previous section we have 'defined' the type `List`, as `List = {null}` $\uplus$ (`int` $\times$ `List`). The fact that `List` appears on the right side of the = sign means that its definition is recursive. Again, recursive definitions appear to be circular, and one way to avoid this circularity is to read the proposition `List` `= {null}` $\uplus$ (`int` $\times$ `List`), not as a definition, but as an equation. The type `List` is therefore defined as the solution to the equation `List = {null}` $\uplus$ (`int` $\times$ `List`). This calls into question the existence and the uniqueness of this solution.

To construct a solution we proceed, as was the case with recursive functions, by successive approximations, by defining the set L_i of values of type `List` that we can construct in at most i steps.

$L_0 = \varnothing$
$L_1 = \{null\} \uplus (int \times L_0) = \{null\}$
$L_2 = \{null\} \uplus (int \times L_1)$
$L_3 = \{null\} \uplus (int \times L_2)$
...

Then, we define the type `List` as the limit of this sequence

$List = \bigcup_i L_i$

The value `null` is essential to this process. The same construction with the equation `List = int × List` gives an empty type.

Note that the type created this way is not a unique solution to the equation `List = {null} ⊎ (int × List)`. The set of all the finite or infinite sequences is also a solution. But the solution created above is the smallest set that is a solution to this equation.

More generally, if you consider a set `E`, a family of sets `A₁, ..., Aₙ` and a family of functions `f₁, ..., fₙ` such that `fᵢ` is an injective function mapping $A_i × E^{m_i}$ to `E` and the images of `fᵢ` are disjoint, you can construct the smallest subset of `E` closed by the functions `fᵢ`. This allows you to understand all recursive type definitions.

Among these recursive types, some have only one recursive field and others have several. We call types with one recursive field *list types*, regardless of the number of non-recursive fields. We call types with several recursive fields *tree types*.

5.1.5 Infinite Values

The type `List` is a solution to the equation `List = {null} ⊎ (int × List)`, but it is not exactly the smallest solution to this equation. Indeed, this type contains values that cannot be constructed in a finite number of steps. For example, the program

```
List l = new List();
l.hd = 4;
l.tl = l;
```

creates the list

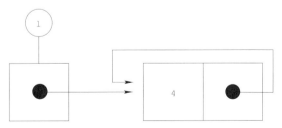

that is, the list `4, 4, 4, 4, 4, ...` which is not really finite.

If `u` and `v` are two finite or infinite lists, we say that `v` is a sub-list of `u` if and only if there exists an integer `n` such that `v` is obtained by erasing the `n` first terms of `u`, that is, if for all `i`, `i` is in the domain of `v` if and only if `i + n` is in the domain of `u` and `vᵢ = uᵢ₊ₙ`.

A list is called *regular* if it has a finite number of sub-lists. For example, the list 4, 4, 4, 4, 4, ... is regular, as is the list 4, 5, 4, 5, 4, 5, 4, 5, 4, 5, ... or the list 1, 2, 3, 4, 5, 4, 5, 4, 5, 4, 5, 4, 5, ... but the list 3, 1, 4, 1, 5, 9, 2, 6, 5, 3, 5, 8, 9, ... is not. It isn't difficult to show that a list is regular if it is either finite, or infinite but ultimately periodic, and that a list of digits of a real number is regular if this number is rational. We can show that the set of regular lists is also a solution to the equation List = {null} ⊎ (int × List). It is this set, and not the set of finite lists, that the declaration of the type List defines. The minimal number of cells for constructing a list is the number of its distinct sub-lists.

This notion of regular lists can be generalised to any recursive type, and we can show that the values of such a type are regular.

Some programmers choose to never create infinite objects. Some programming languages do not even allow the creation of such objects. For example, if you add to Java the binary constructor for lists, you cannot construct infinite lists, because in an expression new List(x,l); the object l must already be created.

It is important to know which convention is in use: allowing or prohibiting the construction of infinite objects, because the function

```
static int sum (final List l) {
  if (l == null) return 0;
  return l.hd + sum(l.tl);}
```

terminates properly if you apply it to finite lists, but enters an infinite loop if you try to apply it to infinite lists.

Exercise 5.2

Write a function that tests whether a regular list is finite or infinite.

5.2 Disjunctive Types

Often, we want to define a type, not as a cartesian product, but as a disjoint union of cartesian products. For example, as we have seen, the type List is defined, not as the cartesian product int × List, but as the disjointed union of the singleton {null} and this cartesian product. Such a type is called a *disjunctive* type.

Another example is that of *arithmetical expressions*. An arithmetical expression is either a constant, for example 3, or a variable, for example x, or the sum of two arithmetical expressions, for example y + 3 or x + (y + 3), or the product of two arithmetical expressions, for example, x × (y + 3).

Based on this fact, we define the type `Expr` by

$$\texttt{Expr = int} \uplus \texttt{String} \uplus \texttt{(Expr} \times \texttt{Expr)} \uplus \texttt{(Expr} \times \texttt{Expr)}$$

When a type can be defined, possibly recursively, as a disjoint union of a singleton and a cartesian product, we identify the singleton element with the value `null`. This method works, for example, with lists, or binary trees `Tree = {leaf}` $\uplus$ `(Tree` $\times$ `Tree)` but not for the type of arithmetical expressions.

Another solution is to place the type inside a larger type that contains a field called the *selector field* that you can, for example, name `select` and that indicates the case in which we find ourselves: constant, variable, sum, or product. And we add enough fields to cover all these cases. In the example of arithmetical expressions, it requires a field of type `int` that is used in the case where the expression is a constant, a field of type `String` that is used in the case where the expression is a variable, and two fields of type `Expr` that are used in the cases where the expression is a sum or a product. This brings us to the following definition.

```
class Expr {
 int select;
 int val;
 String var;
 Expr arg1;
 Expr arg2;}
```

When the value of the selector field is 0, that is, the expression is a constant, we fill in the extra fields, `var`, `arg1` and `arg2` with 'dummy' values, for example `""`, `null` and `null`. Note that it is important that these values exist, that is to say that the corresponding types are not empty. In particular, the type `Expr` must not be empty. In Java, all record types are non-empty as they contain the value `null`.

Exercise 5.3

1. Write a function that takes an arithmetical expression, and outputs it in traditional mathematical notation, with parentheses.

2. Modify this function to eliminate unnecessary parentheses.

Exercise 5.4

Write a function that takes an arithmetical expression and a variable as arguments and computes the derivative of this expression with respect to this variable.

Exercise 5.5

Write a function that takes an arithmetical expression as an argument, and simplifies it using the following simplification rules.

$$e + 0 \longrightarrow e$$
$$0 + e \longrightarrow e$$
$$e \times 0 \longrightarrow 0$$
$$0 \times e \longrightarrow 0$$
$$e \times 1 \longrightarrow e$$
$$1 \times e \longrightarrow e$$

Exercise 5.6

Write a function that tests the equality of two arithmetical expressions.

Exercise 5.7

Define a type for large integers, represented as a list of digits, each digit being of type `int`. Program the four basic operations for these integers.

5.3 Dynamic Data Types and Computability

We have defined, in Exercise 1.12, the notion of a computable function by imagining a fictional type that can contain an integer of arbitrary size. Large integers, defined as lists — and not as arrays — of digits, comes close to this, as their size is only bounded by the size of the memory of the computer in which the program executes. We can show that for a given program and given data, there always exists a certain size of memory sufficient to execute this program using this data.

Adding other dynamic data types does not allow you to compute more functions. This is due to the fact that using a bijection between $\mathbb{N}$ and $\mathbb{N}^2$, it is, in theory, possible to encode any dynamic data as a large integer. Said another way, having either large integers or having all dynamic data types is equivalent from the point of view of computability.

5.4 Caml

In Caml, you can define a recursive record type, for example

```
type list = {hd : int; tl : list;}
```

However, as there is no `null` *value, the smallest solution of this definition is empty. Thus these types contain only infinite values.*

We must therefore specify the disjoint union between the singleton {empty} and the cartesian product int × list *explicitly. A solution is to use a selector field*

```
type list = {select : bool; hd : int; tl : list;}
```

but a default value for the type list *is required in the case of the empty list, and again, there is no* null *value in Caml. The only solution would be to use an infinite default value, which would not be very elegant.*

To solve this problem, Caml has a primitive construct that allows the construction of disjoint unions of cartesian products. The disjoint union of the types $T_1^1 \times \ldots \times T_{n_1}^1, \ldots, T_1^p \times \ldots \times T_{n_p}^p$ *is defined by*

```
type T = C₁ of T₁¹ * ... * T¹ₙ₁ | ... | Cₚ of T₁ᵖ * ... * Tᵖₙₚ
```

where $C_1, \ldots, C_p$ *are constants that replace the selector field values, and that are called* constructors, *although they have little to do with constructors in Java.*

For example, the disjoint union of a singleton — empty cartesian product — and of the cartesian product int × list *is defined below*

```
type list = Nil | Cons of int * list

let l = Cons (5,Cons (4,Nil))
in print_list l
```

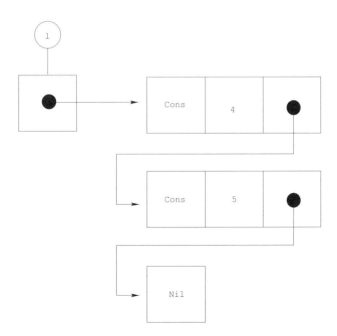

5.5 C

In Java, the value of an expression of a record type is a reference associated in memory with a record. In C, in comparison, the value of such an expression is the record itself. Because of this, in C, there is no value null *and a recursive record type like*

```
struct List {
 int hd;
 struct List tl;};
```

is empty, as a value of this type would contain a field hd *and a field* tl *that would itself contain a field* hd *and a field* tl, *... The definition of such a type is thus prohibited in C.*

The solution to define a type of lists is, as in Java, that the value of the record's second field is, not a record, but a reference associated in memory with a record. But what is implicit in Java must be explicitly stated in C.

```
struct List {
 int hd;
 struct List* tl;};
```

In Java, the contents of the field tl *can be either* null, *or a reference. In C, it is always a reference, but there is a special reference called* NULL *that can never be associated in memory and that plays the same role as* null *in Java. However, this* NULL *construct is not part of the fragment of the language that handles records, but is part of the fragment that handles references, like the constructs* &, *, *... We can therefore construct the following singleton list*

```
struct List l = {3,NULL};
```

Note that the state constructed in C is

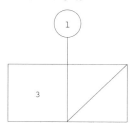

and not as in Java

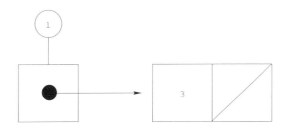

To construct a list of two elements

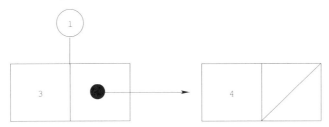

it is necessary to be able to create a cell. For this, there is a counterpart to the new *statement in Java, but that is, once again, independent of records.*

    To allocate a cell, in C, we use the function malloc. *And we create the above list as follows*

```
struct List l;
l.hd = 3;
l.tl = (struct List *) malloc (sizeof(struct List));
(*(l.tl)).hd = 4;
(*(l.tl)).tl = NULL;
```

It is more uniform to put the first element of a list in its own cell. This results in the following state

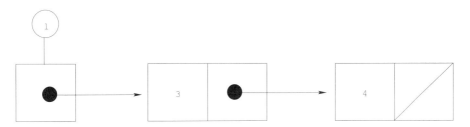

in which the variable l *is, not of type* List, *but of type* List*.

```
struct List* l;
l = (struct List *) malloc (sizeof(struct List));
(*l).hd = 3;
```

```
(*l).tl = (struct List *) malloc (sizeof(struct List));
(*((*l).tl)).hd = 4;
(*((*l).tl)).tl = NULL;
```

The List type of Java corresponds, not to the type List, but to the type List* of C.

5.6 Garbage Collection

5.6.1 Inaccessible Cells

In the state composed of the environment $e = [x = r_1, y = r_4]$ and of the memory state $m = [r_1 = r_2, r_2 = \{hd = 1, tl = r_3\}, r_3 = \{hd = 2, tl = null\}, r_4 = r_5, r_5 = \{hd = 3, tl = r_6\}, r_6 = \{hd = 4, tl = null\}]$

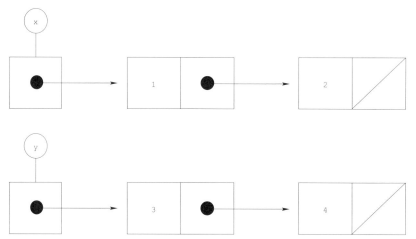

when you execute the statement $y = null;$, we associate the value null with the reference r_4. The memory state now becomes $m' = [r_1 = r_2, r_2 = \{hd = 1, tl = r_3\}, r_3 = \{hd = 2, tl = null\}, r_4 = null, r_5 = \{hd = 3, tl = r_6\}, r_6 = \{hd = 4, tl = null\}]$

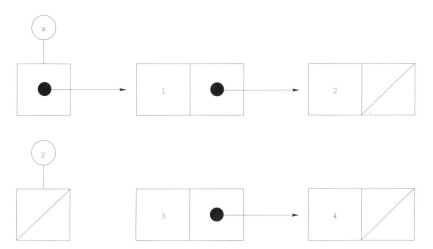

The reference r_5 is not associated with a variable in the environment, and it is not used by any value in memory. It can be removed from memory, which results in m'' = [r_1 = r_2, r_2 = {hd = 1, tl = r_3}, r_3 = {hd = 2, tl = null}, r_4 = null, r_6 = {hd = 4, tl = null}]

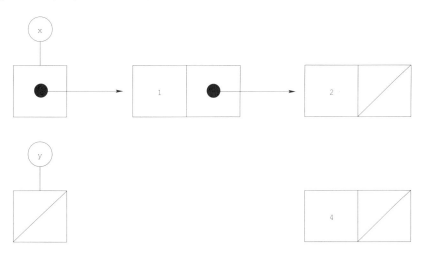

It is then the reference r_6 that can be removed from memory that becomes m''' = [r_1 = r_2, r_2 = {hd = 1, tl = r_3}, r_3 = {hd = 2, tl = null}, r_4 = null]

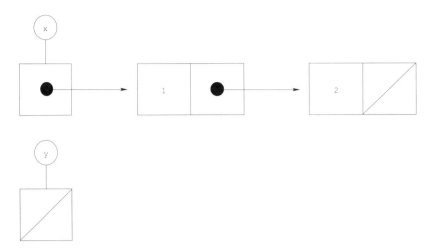

It's not very hard to show that the presence or the absence of these two cells in memory has no *observable effect*. That is, the execution of any program will produce the same results whether these cells are present in memory or not, with the condition that the set of references is infinite.

Each of these cells occupy a certain number of elements in the physical memory of the computer on which the programme is run, that is always finite, and we may want to remove them to economise this memory space: if we did not recycle the physical memory of the computer, we would quickly run out of memory.

Some languages, like Java and Caml, have an automated system of collecting these cells: *garbage collection* (GC).

5.6.2 Programming without Garbage Collection

Other older languages, like C, do not have garbage collection. The memory must therefore be managed by hand. This requires the addition of the references r_5 *and* r_6 *to a list of* free cells *before issuing the statement* y = NULL;.

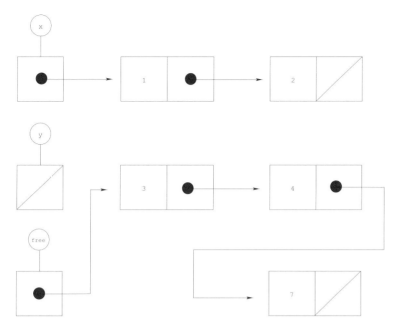

Then, each time you require a new cell, instead of allocating systematically, you can test the `free` *list first to see if it contains a cell, and if it does, you can recycle it.*

When we free a cell, care must be taken that the cell is not still accessible because it was previously shared. If we execute the statement `y = NULL;` *in the state* e = [x = r_1,y = r_4], m = [r_1 = r_2, r_2 = {hd = 1, tl = r_3}, r_3 = {hd = 2, tl = NULL}, r_4 = r_5, r_5 = {hd = 3, tl = r_3}]

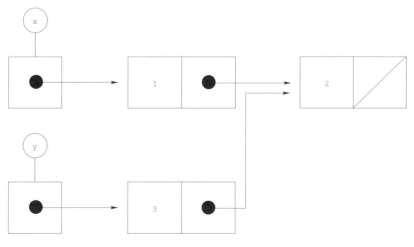

we obtain the state

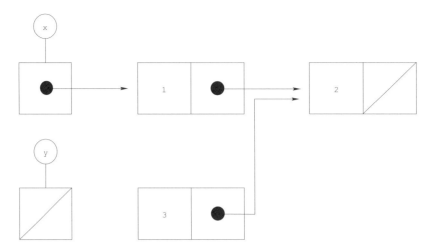

in which we can free the cell r_5 but not the cell r_3, which appears not only in the pair associated with the reference r_5 but also in the pair associated with the reference r_2.

This requires that information about the number of times that the reference r_3 is used in memory be available in the cell r_3. Therefore, we add to each cell a field that contains an integer indicating the number of occurrences of this cell in the memory and the environment. This field is called a reference counter. *In the above example, the reference counter of the cell r_5 is* 1 *and the reference counter of the cell r_3 is* 2. *Before executing the statement* y = NULL; *we decrement the reference counter of r_5 which becomes* 0, *which means that the cell can be collected. Collecting this cell decrements the reference counter of r_3 which becomes* 1, *but this cell is not collected.*

The C language contains a statement free *that manages a list of free cells automatically, but the decision to free a cell or not is always up to the programmer.*

5.6.3 Global Methods of Memory Management

In some languages, like Java and Caml, garbage collection is automatic, and the programmer does not have to worry about it. Local methods, like using a reference counter, were used by early languages as a means of managing the memory, but they have been replaced by global methods, like using a *marking*.

At some point, the execution of the program stops and all its accessible references in the environment are recursively marked with a star

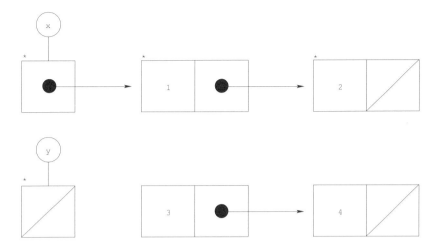

then the physical memory of the computer is scanned, all the non-marked cells are collected and the execution of the program resumes.

An advantage of these global methods is that they only require the addition of a boolean to each cell, and not the addition of an integer for reference counting. Also, they allow you to free more cells when using infinite values. For instance, in the following state

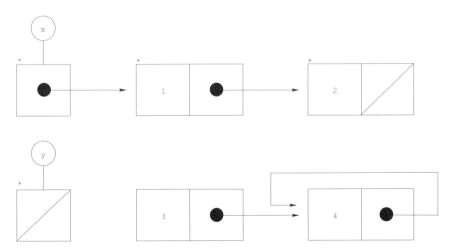

only one cell is collected using a reference counter, but two are with the markup method.

5.6.4 Garbage Collection and Functions

Garbage collection has a subtle interaction with function calls. Indeed, when you start the garbage collection during the execution of a function, it is possible that some variables are not in the current environment but will return to the environment when the function returns. This typically occurs with local variables of the main program.

The initial set of references to mark is not only the set of references accessible in the current environment, but the set of accessible references of all the environments of functions in which you may return after finishing execution of the current function.

6
Programming with Lists

6.1 Finite Sets and Functions of a Finite Domain

6.1.1 Membership

Imagine that all the libraries in a city or a country decide to consolidate their catalogs together and write a program that allows you to know which book is in which library, allowing for inter-library loans.

The users of this program have the option of asking whether a certain book is in a certain library or not. For this, a function must be written that takes a character string s and a list of character strings b as arguments, and returns the boolean value `true` or `false` depending on whether the string s appears in the list b or not.

This function can be written as follows

```
static boolean mem (String s, List b) {
 if (b == null) return false;
 if (equal(s,b.hd)) return true;
 return mem(s,b.tl);}
```

Then, you can define a list

```
List b = new List("Discourse on the Method",
        new List("Critique of Pure Reason",
        new List("Principles of Programming Languages",
        null)));
```

G. Dowek, *Principles of Programming Languages,*
Undergraduate Topics in Computer Science, DOI 10.1007/978-1-84882-032-6_6,
© Springer-Verlag London Limited 2009

and use the function

```
System.out.println(mem("Discourse on the Method",b));
```

The program would then output `true`.

The function `mem` above is recursive. It is also possible to use a `while` loop

```
static boolean mem (String s, List b) {
 while (b != null) {if (equal(s,b.hd)) return true; b = b.tl;}
 return false;}
```

Exercise 6.1

How many operations occur when searching an element in a list? How many operations occur when adding a new element to a list? How many operations occur when removing an element from a list?

Exercise 6.2

A *multiset* is a set in which an element can appear more than once. It is thus formally a function that maps a set to the set of natural numbers, which associates each element with its multiplicity. We can represent finite multisets as lists, allowing repetition.

Write a function that takes two lists as arguments and computes the cardinality of the intersection of the two multisets represented by these lists.

Write a function that takes two lists as arguments and computes the number of elements that appear in the same place in both lists.

Write a program that plays Mastermind. The computer creates a list of n randomly chosen pegs from p colours. For each turn, the computer asks the user to enter a list of the same format. The computer then outputs the number of pegs in the correct position, and the number of correct pegs in an incorrect position.

6.1.2 Association Lists

An *association list* is a list of pairs that is functional, meaning that for each k, there exists at most one element v such that the pair (k,v) appears in the list. The first element of a pair in the list is called a *key* and the second is called a *value*. Association lists are a means of representing functions of a finite domain, like dictionaries.

Exercise 6.3

Write a function that searches for a key in an association list and returns the value associated with this key.

Write a function that updates an association list, so that the value associated with a key is updated if it already exists, and is added if not.

6.2 Concatenation: Modify or Copy

6.2.1 Modify

Imagine that two libraries decided to merge. To create the new library's catalog, a new list must be created that contains the elements from both libraries. This operation, which begins with two lists x_1, ..., x_n and y_1, ..., y_p, creates the list x_1, ..., x_n, y_1, ..., y_p is called *concatenation*. To simplify our diagrams, we will consider lists of characters instead of lists of character strings. Concatenation can be programmed as follows

```
static List append (List x, List y) {
 if (x == null) return y;
 List p = x;
 while (p.tl != null) p = p.tl;
 p.tl = y;
 return x;}
```

If you define two lists

```
List b = new List('a',new List('p',new List('p', null)));
List c = new List('e',new List('n',new List('d', null)));
```

and you output their concatenation

```
printList(append(b,c));
```

you obtain the list

```
a p p e n d
```

Indeed, in the case where the list x is not empty, the statement p = x; starts by putting the first element of the list x in the variable p

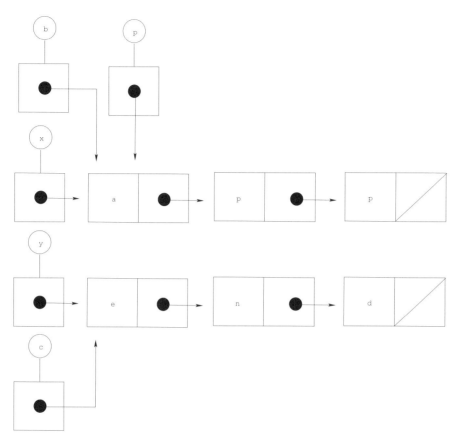

Then the statement `while (p.tl != null) p = p.tl;` shifts this reference in such a way that the variable `p` contains the last cell in the list

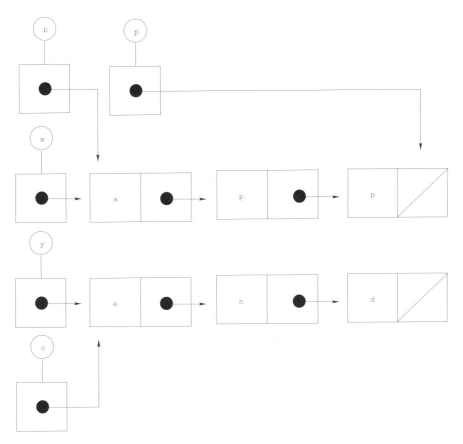

Then, the statement `p.tl = y;` replaces the field `tl` of this cell by the first cell in the list `y`

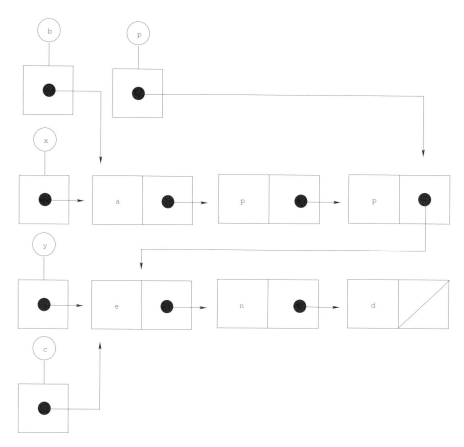

And finally the statement `return x;` returns the first cell of the list `x`. The value returned by the function is then the first cell of a list whose elements are a p p e n d.

However, this function is not perfect, because if, after the computation, you output the list `b` and the list `c` you obtain e n d for the list `c` but a p p e n d and not a p p for the list `b`. As you can see in the figure, the variable `b` also contains the first cell of a list whose elements are a p p e n d.

In addition, the result of this function is not the concatenation of its two arguments when both lists have elements in common. When you concatenate `b` and `b` for example, you place the first cell of the list `b` in the field `tl` of the last cell of this list and you construct an infinite list. The statement

```
printList(append(b,b));
```

outputs

```
a p p a p p a p p a p p ...
```

Thus, this function has the benefit of not allocating extra cells, which is desirable when the lists are very long, but at the expense of modifying its arguments, and not being correct when its arguments share cells.

Exercise 6.4

How many distinct sublists does the list a b c have? What about the list a b c a b c a b c a b c a b c ...? And the list a b c a b c? Show that if f is an arbitrary function that does not allocate memory, and that l is the list a b c then f(l,l) cannot return the list a b c a b c.

6.2.2 Copy

An alternative is the following function

```
static List append (List x, List y) {
 if (x == null) return y;
 else {
  List p = x;
  List q = new List(x.hd,null);
  List r = q;
  while (p.tl != null)
   {q.tl = new List(p.tl.hd,null); q = q.tl;p = p.tl;}
  q.tl = y;
  return r;}}
```

In this case, we copy the list x to a list r, and we put the first cell of the list y in the tl field of the last element of list r. This results in the following

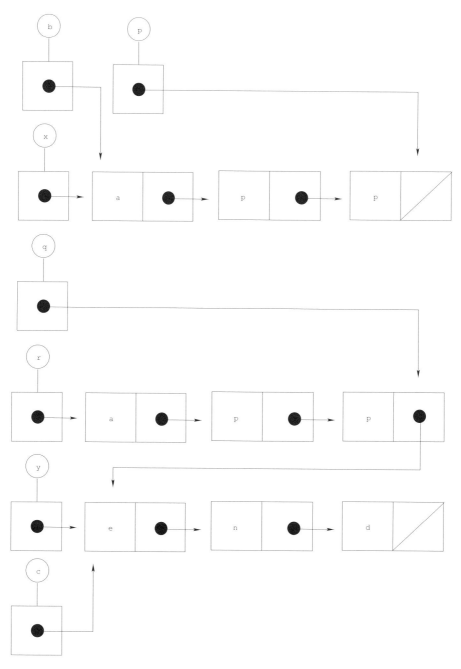

and the variable b keeps the value a p p. The advantage of this function is
that it does not alter its arguments and that it can be applied to any two lists,
even if they have elements in common. However, it does this with the added

expense of having to create a copy of its first argument.

Exercise 6.5

What happens to the diagrams above when the elements of the list are not of a scalar type, but of a composite type, like a character string?

6.2.3 Using Recursion

Instead of using a `while` loop, you can program concatenation by copying its first argument recursively

```
static List append (List x, List y) {
  if (x == null) return y;
  return new List(x.hd, append(x.tl,y));}
```

In this case, assignment is not used and the function is written in the functional core of Java.

6.2.4 Chemical Reactions and Mathematical Functions

The choice between these different methods of programming concatenation illustrates a decision that frequently presents itself when writing programs: modifying the data or copying it. This difference is similar to that between a chemical reaction and a mathematical function. In mathematics, if we state that $x = 32$ and then apply the function $y \mapsto y + 1$ to x, we obtain the result 33, but the variable x retains the value 32, so that we can later apply the function $y \mapsto 2 \times y$ to x and obtain the result 64. We can also apply the + function to the variables x and x. The variable x is a cornucopia of 32's.

In chemistry, in contrast, when a molecule of oxygen and two molecules of hydrogen react to form two molecules of water, the oxygen and hydrogen molecules are consumed by the reaction and cannot be reused for another reaction. In addition, the hydrogen molecules must be distinct: a molecule cannot react with itself. Nothing is lost, and nothing is created, and there are no cornucopias.

When we work with a small amount of data, it is always preferable to copy it. This allows you to treat the function **append** as a mathematical function and to avoid having to worry about whether or not the data has been altered by another function. In contrast, when working with large amounts of data, copying the data becomes unfeasible. For example, when updating a database, you must accept that the state of the database will change and that the old state will be lost.

Exercise 6.6

Program a function that removes an element from a list, by copying its argument. Create another function that does the same, but by modifying its argument.

Exercise 6.7 (Sieve of Eratosthenes)

Consider lists of pairs formed of an integer and a boolean that indicates whether this integer is marked or not.

1. Write a function that marks all the elements in positions that are non-trivial multiples of an integer `n` in a list `l`.

2. Write a function that returns the list of integers between 2 ... 1000 none of them being marked.

3. Write a function that returns the list of prime numbers below 1000.

Exercise 6.8

If `T` is a type that can be mathematically ordered, such as integers, we say that a list of elements of type `T` is *ordered* if each element of this list is of lesser value than the next.

1. Write a function that tests whether a list is ordered or not

2. Write two functions that insert an element to and remove an element from an ordered list.

Exercise 6.9

A polynomial can be represented by a functional list of pairs composed of an exponent and a coefficient, ordered by increasing exponent. Write a function that computes the sum of two polynomials.

6.3 List Inversion: an Extra Argument

The inverse of a list $x_1, \ldots, x_n$ is $x_n, \ldots, x_1$. You can program a function that reverses a list quite easily using recursion, since, if the list `l` is non-empty, its inverse is obtained by adding `l.hd` to the end of the inverse of `l.tl`.

```
static List reverse (final List x) {
 if (x == null) return null;
 return add(reverse(x.tl),x.hd);}
```

where the function `add` is defined by

```
static List add (final List x, final int y) {
  if (x == null) return new List(y,null);
  return new List(x.hd,add(x.tl,y));}
```

To add an element to the end of a list of n elements, the function add must complete a number of operations linear in n. To reverse a list of n elements, the function reverse requires a number of operations linear in 1 + 2 + ... + n, which is asymptotically equivalent to k n^2, for some non zero constant k.

The *time complexity*, or simply *complexity*, of a program is the number of operations that a particular program executes, as a function of the size of its given data. In the case of the reverse function, the number of operations depends only on the size n of the list to reverse. In other cases, the number of operations required may be dependent on other factors. We distinguish these two types of complexity: the *worst case complexity*, which is a function that maps n to the maximum number of operations the program requires for data of size n, and the *average complexity*, which is the function that maps n to the mean number of operations the program requires for all possible types of data of size n.

The complexity of the reverse function is asymptotically equivalent to k n^2, for some non zero constant k, and we say that this function's complexity is *quadratic* with respect to the size of the list.

However, we know that it is possible to reverse the order of a deck of cards in linear time

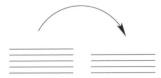

since, in n operations, we can move each card from the pile on the left to the pile on the right. At the end, the card on top of the pile on the left will be on the bottom of the pile on the right.

This method is linear because we have two places to store cards: the left pile and the right pile. To write a function reverse that is linear, we must use the same idea, by writing a function revappend with two arguments x and y — analogous to the left hand pile and the right hand pile — that computes the concatenation of the inverse of x with y

```
static List revappend (final List x, final List y) {
  if (x == null) return y;
  return revappend(x.tl,new List(x.hd,y));}
```

```
static List reverse (final List x) {
  return revappend(x,null);}
```

Exercise 6.10

Write a function `reverse` that modifies its arguments and does not allocate memory.

Exercise 6.11 (The Cartesian Product of a Family of Sets)

Consider a list l_0, l_1, l_2, ... such that each l_i is itself a list. Print all the lists that can be obtained by taking an element in l_0, an element in l_1, ...

6.4 Lists and Arrays

We have seen that a list, like an array, is a tuple of objects of the same type. Each time you want to use a tuple of objects in a program, you can choose to use a list or an array.

An advantage of an array is that it allows you to directly access its data: accessing the nth element of an array occurs in constant time, if n is of a scalar type like `int` and a time proportional to the number of digits of n, that is of the logarithm of n, if we replace this scalar type with a type of large integers — which is required to conceptualise n tending towards infinity. Accessing the nth elements of a list, in contrast, occurs in linear time with respect to n.

The advantage of a list is that its size does not need to be known in advance, and lists used with recursively defined functions that copy their arguments allow you to use the functional core of the language in question. Data is therefore never altered. It can be used any number of times. And functions resemble mathematical functions: they take an object as an argument, return another object, and do not alter any object already in existence.

Put more simply, we can say that lists allow for simpler programs, but arrays allow for more efficient ones.

6.5 Stacks and Queues

In mathematics, equipping the same set with different operations produces different structures. Likewise, with programming languages, lists, stacks and queues are three structures which are composed of similar elements, but whose operations are different. The operations on lists are

1. Creating an empty list,

2. Testing to see if a list is empty,

3. Creating a list whose head is the object x and whose tail is the list l,

4. Accessing the head of a list,

5. Accessing the tail of a list,

6. Modifying the head of a list,

7. Modifying the tail of a list.

6.5.1 Stacks

The operations on stacks are

1. Creating an empty stack,

2. Testing to see if a stack is empty,

3. Adding — pushing — an element onto the stack,

4. Accessing the top element on the stack,

5. Removing — popping — the top element off the stack.

The first element of a stack is called the *top* and not the head of the stack, since it can be thought of as a vertical pile, like a stack of plates. The operation that removes the top element can be thought of as returning the tail of a list, but the difference is that the statement l2 = l1.tl; does not modify the list l1, while the statement pop(p);, which removes the top of the stack p, modifies that stack.

Because this statement modifies its argument, it is necessary to represent a stack, not as a list, but as a list inside a wrapper

```
class List {
 int hd;
 List tl;

 List (final int x, final List y) {this.hd = x; this.tl = y;}}

class Stack  {
 List c;

 Stack (final List x) {this.c = x;}}
```

And we program the five operations above as follows

```
static Stack empty () {
 return new Stack(null);}

static boolean testempty (final Stack l) {
 return l.c == null;}

static void push (final int a, final Stack l) {
 l.c = new List(a,l.c);}

static void pop (final Stack l) {
 l.c = l.c.tl;}

static int top (final Stack l) {
 return l.c.hd;}
```

We can then use these operations, for example in the following program

```
public static void main (String [] args) {
 Stack p = empty ();
 push(4,p);
 push(5,p);
 System.out.println(top(p));
 pop(p);
 System.out.println(testempty(p));
 System.out.println(top(p));}
```

which outputs 5, false, and 4.

Exercise 6.12

The *postfix* notation is a notation for arithmetical expressions in which you write 3 4 + instead of writing 3 + 4: you write the two arguments of a function before the function itself. An advantage of this notation is that it does not require parentheses. For example, the expression (3 + 4) + 5 is written 3 4 + 5 +, while the expression 3 + (4 + 5) is written 3 4 5 + +.

1. How would you write the expression 3 + (4 + (5 + (6 + (7 + (8 + 9))))) using postfix notation?

2. Consider the expression 3 4 5 6 7 8 9 + + + + + + as a list of elements, thirteen in this case, such that each element is either a constant or the symbol of a mathematical operation. Define a type for these postfix arithmetical expressions.

3. We evaluate a postfix arithmetical expression using a stack. We read the elements of the expression from left to right. When we read a constant, we add it to the top of the stack. When we read an operator symbol, we pop the top of the stack twice, and add to the stack a new element that is the result of applying the operation to the two popped numbers. Show that reading a complete expression adds to the stack a unique element that is the value of this expression.

4. Program in Java a function that reads a postfix expression and computes its value.

Exercise 6.13 (Eliminating Recursion)

A recursive program can always be transformed into a non-recursive one by using a stack. As an example, we will transform the program of Exercise 3.5, which solves the Towers of Hanoi, into a program that does not use recursion.

To move a group of k disks from column x to column y, we start by moving k - 1 disks of column x towards column m, and 1 disk of column x towards column y and finally k - 1 disks from column m towards column y, where m is the column different from x and y. This can be programmed recursively

```
static void h (final int x, final int y, final int k) {
 if (k == 1) System.out.print(x + " -> " + y + "   ");
 else {int m = 6 - (x + y);
       h(x,m,k - 1);
       h(x,y,1);
       h(m,y,k - 1);}}
```

An alternative to using recursion is to use a stack that contains the set of movements of groups of disks waiting to be executed. Each movement is described by a triplet of integers composed of the origin of the group, its destination, and the number of disks in the group.

As long as the stack is not empty, we examine its top. If it describes the movement of a group composed of a single disk, we output the movement of this disk and we remove the top of the stack. If it contains a movement of a group composed of k disks, we replace it with three descriptions of movements of smaller groups.

Write a program that solves the Tower of Hanoi without using recursion.

Exercise 6.14

We consider a list of characters in the set '(', ')', '[', ']'. The set of well formatted lists is the smallest set such that

– the empty list is well formatted,

– if l is well formatted then so are (l) and [l],

– if l_1 and l_2 are well formatted then so is l_1 l_2.

For example, the list ([[()]()][]) is well formatted, but the list ([[()](]][]) is not.

Write a function that indicates whether or not a list of characters is well formatted of not.

For once, it is easier to use a stack than recursion.

6.5.2 Queues

The operations on queues are

1. Creating an empty queue,

2. Testing to see if a queue is empty or not,

3. Adding an element to the end of a queue,

4. Accessing to an element from the front of the queue,

5. Removing an element from the front of the queue.

The only difference between a stack and queue is that we add elements to the end of a queue while we add elements to the beginning of a stack: queues are first come, first serve. Queues are also sometimes called *fifo: first in, first out.*

Exercise 6.15

Program the above operations by using an wrapper containing a list to represent queues. What is the time complexity of adding an element?

Exercise 6.16

To make the operation that adds an element faster, we can represent a queue for which we know ahead of time the maximum size max by an array of size max. The elements of a queue of size n are placed in the i % max cell, (i + 1) % max, ... (i + n - 1) % max for an integer i.

Program the above operations for this data structure.

Exercise 6.17

To make the operation that adds an element faster, we can also represent a queue by two lists. The pair composed of the lists $l_1, \ldots, l_p$ and $m_1, \ldots, m_q$ represents the queue $l_1, \ldots, l_p, m_q, \ldots, m_1$.

Program the above operations for this data structure.

What is the time complexity for the operation that accesses the first element in the best case? In the worst case? In the average case?

6.5.3 Priority Queues

In a hospital's emergency room, a first come, first serve policy is not always optimal. A better solution is to assign each patient a priority level and to serve the patients with a higher priority first.

The operations on priority queues are

1. Creating an empty queue,

2. Testing to see if the queue is empty or not,

3. Adding an element to a queue,

4. Accessing to the next element with the highest priority,

5. Removing the next element with the highest priority.

Exercise 6.18

Program the operations above by representing a priority queue with a list and by adding new elements to the head.

What is the time complexity of the operation that adds an element to the queue? And that of the operation that reads the element with the highest priority?

And what if we represent a priority queue with a list ordered by decreasing priority?

7
Exceptions

7.1 Exceptional Circumstances

We have seen that when we represent a finite set with a list, in order to test the membership of an element in the set, we use a function called `mem` such that the value of the expression `mem(x,l)` is either `true` or `false` depending on whether the element `x` appears in the list or not.

Similarly, when we represent a function of a finite domain with an association list, to obtain the element associated with a key, we use a function called `assoc` such that the value of the expression `assoc(x,l)` is the value associated with the key `x` in the list `l`. But what should the function `assoc` return when the key `x` is not in the list `l`? There are several possible solutions.

– We can return a default value. If possible, this default value should be disjoint from the image of the function, and is typically `-1`.

– We can return a pair composed of a boolean indicating if the key is in the domain of the function and a value that is the value associated with that key when the boolean is equal to `true` and a default value when it is equal to `false`.

– We can return an element of a disjunctive type, the disjoint union of a singleton and of the type of values.

– We can decide to never use the function `assoc` when the key does not exist in the list. To do this, we can write a function called `domain` that returns a

G. Dowek, *Principles of Programming Languages*,
Undergraduate Topics in Computer Science, DOI 10.1007/978-1-84882-032-6_7,
© Springer-Verlag London Limited 2009

boolean indicating whether or not a key is in the domain of the function and we always use the `domain` function before using the `assoc` function.

Each of these solutions has shortcomings: the first solution uses a value to symbolise the absence of a value, which is somewhat ambiguous and not immediately clear. The second and third cause the `assoc` function to have a more complex type. And the last solution requires the association list to be traversed twice.

7.2 Exceptions

An alternative solution is to use a construct called an *exception*. We could use an exception in the `assoc` function as follows

```
static int assoc (final int x, final List l) throws Exception {
 if (l == null) throw new Exception();
 if (x == l.key) return l.val;
 return assoc(x,l.tl);}
```

This function is a partial function that returns the value associated with the key `x` in the list `l` when this value exists and that fails otherwise. In this case, we say that the function *raises* an exception. The statement to raise an exception is `throw e;` where `e` is a value of type `Exception`. The simplest method of creating a value of type `Exception` is to use the `new` construct: `new Exception();`.

The fact that the function `assoc` can raise an exception must be declared by adding `throws Exception` between the list of arguments and the body of the function. Care must be taken to not confuse the keyword `throw`, used to throw an exception, and the keyword `throws`, used to indicate that an exception can be thrown.

7.3 Catching Exceptions

When we call a function that can raise an exception, we can specify what we would like to happen when this function raises an exception. This is done with the construct `try p catch (Exception e) q;`, for example

```
try {System.out.println(assoc(x,l));}
catch (Exception e) {System.out.println("Not in the list");}
```

When we execute such a statement, we start by executing the statement p. If the execution of this statement raises an exception, then execution of the statement p is interrupted and the statement q is executed. Thus, if x is a key of l, we output the value associated with this key, and if this isn't the case, we output the character string "Not in the list".

In this example, all the exceptions cause the instruction System.out.println("Not in the list"); to be executed. It is also possible, in Java, to define different exceptions and to execute this statement only when one particular exception is raised.

In a sequence of statements {p₁ p₂}, if the statement p_1 raises an exception, then the statement p_2 is not executed. From this point of view, the statement throw resembles the statement return quite a bit.

7.4 The Propagation of Exceptions

We can use the function assoc to write a function called assocplus that returns the value associated with a key in the list, plus 1. Since we are using the function assoc, we must specify what will happen when the function assoc raises an exception. We can, for example, decide that the function assocplus itself raises an exception in this case.

```
static int assocplus
            (final int x, final List l) throws Exception {
 try {return assoc(x,l) + 1;}
 catch (Exception e) {throw e;}}
```

However, it isn't necessary to be this explicit, since if in the function g, we use the function f that can raise an exception, without using a try block, then when f raises an exception, g raises an exception as well. Thus, the function assocplus can be rewritten more simply as

```
static int assocplus
            (final int x, final List l) throws Exception {
 return assoc(x,l) + 1;}
```

And the statement

```
try {System.out.println(assocplus(x,l));}
catch (Exception e) {System.out.println("Not in the list");}
```

outputs the value associated with x in l plus 1 if this key appears in the list, and the character string "Not in the list" otherwise.

The option to let exceptions propagate from function to function is the main advantage of using exceptions instead of returning a boolean with the value associated with the key x. Without the use of exceptions, the function assocplus becomes much more verbose and less elegant

```
static Pair assocplus (final int x, final List l) {
 Pair p = assoc(x,l);
 if (p.b) return new Pair(true,p.v + 1);
 return p;}
```

You can compare the behaviour of the assocplus function when the key is not in the list to that of a student when the fire alarm sounds during a chemistry lab. The procedure, when we hear a fire alarm, is to exit the building immediately. But the lab instructions require you to mix two chemicals, A and B, in a test tube, and to heat the mixture, then add a third product C, saying nothing about fire alarms. The lab instructions would become much more difficult to read if they read "If the fire alarm rings, then exit the building, otherwise mix chemicals A and B, and if the fire alarm rings, then exit the building, otherwise heat the mixture, and if the fire alarm rings, then..."

7.5 Error Messages

Some primitives in Java can throw exceptions. The statement

```
System.out.println(1/0);
```

throws the exception

```
java.lang.ArithmeticException: / by zero
```

Error messages in Java are then simply a particular case of exceptions.

7.6 The Semantics of Exceptions

Defining the Σ function in a language that has exceptions requires some work. We have seen that the result of the execution of a statement had a first component that was either return or normal depending on whether the execution of this statement encountered a return statement or not. We now have to add a third case, exception, for the case where the execution of this statement raises an exception. Likewise, the evaluation of an expression can now complete normally or raise an exception.

The exception case is not very different from the return case. In particular, if in a sequence {p₁ p₂} the execution of p₁ raises an exception, then the statement p₂ is not executed and the result of the execution of {p₁ p₂} is this same exception.

Exercise 7.1

Extend the definition of the Σ function to take exceptions into consideration.

7.7 Caml

In Caml, the statement throw e *is written* raise e. *It is not necessary to declare that a function can raise an exception. We declare a new exception with the statement* exception C. *We catch an exception with the construct* try p with _ -> q.

Thus, we can start by declaring an exception

```
exception Not_in_the_list
```

and define the function assoc *and use it in the main program*

```
let rec assoc x l = if l = []
                    then raise Not_in_the_list
                    else if fst(List.hd l) = x
                        then snd(List.hd l)
                        else assoc x (List.tl l)
in try print_int(assoc 5 [(3,4)])
   with _ -> print_string("Not in the list")
```

There are no exceptions in C, *but some constructs like* long jumps *have some similarities.*

8
Objects

The programs we have seen so far have been composed of type declarations, global variable declarations, function definitions, and the main program — the `main` function.

As we have seen, the use of functions allows for a better layout of programs, since a main program of a few thousand lines would be very difficult to read and understand. However, the use of functions isn't sufficient to create extremely long programs that also become difficult to read and understand when they are composed of dozens of functions. Other constructs, such as *modules* and *objects*, allow programs to be even better structured.

8.1 Classes

8.1.1 Functions as Part of a Type

We have seen in Chapter 6 that, in the same way as a mathematical structure is defined not only by a set, but also by operations defined on that set, the concept of a stack or a queue was defined not only by a type, but also by operations on that type. Because of this, it is reasonable to imagine that the functions `push`, `pop`, ... could be part of the definition of the type `Stack`. A type equipped with functions is called a *class* and the functions are called *methods* of the class.

G. Dowek, *Principles of Programming Languages*,
Undergraduate Topics in Computer Science, DOI 10.1007/978-1-84882-032-6_8,
© Springer-Verlag London Limited 2009

So, instead of defining the stack type, plus its functions, plus the main program

```
class Stack  {
 List c;

 Stack ...
}

class Prog {

  static Stack empty ...

  static boolean testempty ...

  static void push ...

  static void pop ...

  static int top ...

  static int f ...

 public static void main (String [] args) ...
}
```

we can place the functions push, pop, ... in the class Stack

```
class Stack  {

 List c;

 Stack ...

 static Stack empty ...

 static boolean testempty ...

 static void push ...

 static void pop ...

 static int top ...
```

```
}

class Prog {

 static int f ...

 public static void main (String [] args) ...
}
```

A class is thus composed of three things: a list of fields, a list of constructors, and a list of methods.

To call the method `push`, instead of writing `push(p);` you write `Stack.push(p);`. It is important to distinguish between the two uses of the `.` symbol: when accessing a field, you use the notation `p.c` where `p` is an expression of type `Stack`, and when you access the method `push`, you use the notation `Stack.push` where `Stack` is the class itself.

When we use a method of a class `T` inside the class itself, then it is not necessary to precede the method name with the class name. Thus, inside the class `Stack`, the name `push` is an abbreviation for the name `Stack.push`.

8.1.2 The Semantics of Classes

To extend the Σ function, it is necessary that, in the list of classes, each class is associated with a triplet composed of a list of fields, a list of constructors, and a list of methods.

Exercise 8.1

Define the Σ function to account for the inclusion of method calls. Assume, for this exercise, that methods cannot access global variables.

8.2 Dynamic Methods

The methods of a class `T` often have an object of the class `T` among their arguments. This is the case, for example, of the methods `push` and `pop` of the class `Stack`. Such a method is called by the statement or the expression `T.f(b_1,...,a,...,b_p)` where `a` is an argument of type `T`.

It is possible, in the definition of a method in the class `T`, to distinguish one special argument of type `T`: we omit the keyword `static` in the method's definition, we do not list it as a formal argument of the method, and in the body of the function we use a special variable called `this`. Then, we call this method not with the statement or the expression $T.f(b_1,\ldots,a,\ldots,b_p)$ but with the statement or the expression $a.f(b_1,\ldots,b_p)$. This type of method is called a *dynamic* method.

For example, instead of defining the methods `push` and `pop` as follows

```
static void push (final int a, final Stack l) {
 l.c = new List(a,l.c);}

static void pop (final Stack l) {
 l.c = l.c.tl;}
```

you can define them more concisely using dynamic methods

```
void push (final int a) {
 this.c = new List(a,this.c);}

void pop () {
 this.c = this.c.tl;}
```

We call these methods with `p.pop(); p.push(5);`. We can then execute the following program

```
Stack p = Stack.empty ();
p.push(5);
p.push(6);
System.out.println(p.top());
p.pop();
System.out.println(p.top());
```

that outputs 6 and 5.

In fact, it is possible to be even more concise, since in the body of a dynamic method of the class `T`, if `c` is a field of the class `T` and there is no local variable with the same name, the expression `c` is an abbreviation for `this.c`. Thus, you can define the methods `push` and `pop` as follows

```
void push (final int a) {
 c = new List(a,c);}

void pop () {
 c = c.tl;}
```

It is important to note that a dynamic method can only be called when the object with which it is called does not have the value `null`. Thus, if `append` is a dynamic method, we can write `l1.append(l2)` only when the list `l1` is non empty. To be able to call the function `append` with an empty list, you must either use a static method, or use a wrapper type. For instance, the empty stack is not represented with the value `null`, but with an object that contains a field `c` whose value is `null`. Because of this, even if the stack `p` is empty, the statement `p.push(5);` is valid and adds the value 5 to the top of the stack `p`.

A common error is to write a dynamic method

```
List f () {
  if (this == null) ...}
```

Basically, the boolean `this == null` will always be equal to `false`, because the method `f` cannot be called when the object is `null`.

The extension of the Σ function to include dynamic methods isn't very difficult, even if care must be taken to avoid confusing the assignment `c = 1;` of the variable `c` with that of the field `c` of the object `this`.

Exercise 8.2

Give the definition of the Σ function, for dynamic methods.

Exercise 8.3 (A Logo Turtle)

On a euclidean plane, a solid object has three degrees of freedom. A Logo turtle is an object with three fields `x`, `y` and `a`. The fields `x` and `y` are the coordinates of the turtle, and `a` is the angle that it forms with the `x` axis.

A turtle has two methods: `forward`, which takes a number `l` as an argument and causes the turtle to move forward by `l` units, and `turn`, which takes a number `b` as an argument and causes the turtle to rotate about its centre by the relative angle `b`. Also, when the turtle advances, it draws a line segment that goes from its departure to its arrival point.

What does the following program draw?

```
for (int i = 0; i < 4; i = i + 1) {r.forward(50); r.turn(90);}
```

Write a program that draws a regular pentagon. Write a program that draws any regular polygon of `n` sides.

Write a program that draws the Koch Snowflake — see Exercise 3.6 — with a turtle.

8.3 Methods and Functional Fields

We can say that a dynamic method is associated, not with a class, but with an object of a class and that when we execute the statement `p.push(5);`, we call the method `push` of the stack `p` and not of the class `Stack`. Thus, we can see the stack `p` as a record that, in addition to its field `c`, has the fields `push`, `pop` that are, not values, but functions. Such a record where certain fields are functions is called an *object* and the functional fields of an object are called methods.

When we see methods as functional fields, we understand that the object `null`, which has no fields, also has no methods.

In principle, in the class `Stack`, two objects `p` and `q` could have methods `push` that are completely different, as they can have fields `c` that are different. However, in Java, the dependence of the method `push` with respect to the object to which it belongs is limited: it's the same function that is executed when you call the method `push` of the stack `p` and the stack `q`, the only difference being that the variable `this` is equal to `p` in the first case and is equal to `q` in the second.

We will see, however, that a construct in Java called *inheritance* allows, in some cases, different objects of the same class to have different methods.

8.4 Static Fields

A dynamic method belongs to an object. A static method, in contrast, belongs to a class. It is the same method for all objects of that class.

Similarly, a field can be static or dynamic. We declare a static field by preceding it with the keyword `static`. When we modify a static field, it is modified for all the class.

So, if we define the class

```
class M {
 static int mem;

 void modify (final int x) {
  mem = x;}
```

```
void print () {
  System.out.println(mem);}}
```

the program

```
M a = new M();
M b = new M();
a.modify(4);
b.modify(5);
a.print();
```

outputs 5 and not 4. Because the field `mem` is static, the body `mem = x;` of the method `modify` is an abbreviation of the statement `M.mem = x;` and not `this.mem = x;`.

8.5 Static Classes

A class is *static* if all its fields and methods are static. Objects of such a class have no fields or methods of their own, so there is no reason to create such objects.

However, static classes are a means of grouping functions that belong together. For example, the class `Math` groups together mathematical functions: `Math.sin`, `Math.cos`, ...

Static classes allow the grouping of functions. In programming languages, a construct that allows the grouping of functions is called a *module*. In Java, static classes play the role of modules.

In Java, a program itself is a static class, which explains why we write `class Prog` at the beginning of the program `Prog`. A program's global variables are simply static fields of this class, which explains why we precede their definitions with the keyword `static`. The functions of the program are methods of this class. The only special requirement of a program class is that it must contain a method called `main`.

We defined in Section 8.1.2 the function Σ of five arguments $\Sigma(\texttt{p,e,m,G,C})$ where `p` is a statement, `e` is an environment, `m` is a memory state, `G` is a global environment and `C` is a list of classes, but we now know that the global environment `G` is simply a class like any other, and that it should be part of the list `C`. The final definition of the Σ function is thus a function of four arguments $\Sigma(\texttt{p,e,m,C})$.

Exercise 8.4

Give the definition of the Σ function while taking into account the fact that the global environment is a class.

8.6 Inheritance

```
class Clock {
 int h;
 int mn;

 Clock () {}

 Clock (final int x, final int y) {h = x; mn = y;}

 void drawDial (final int x, final int y, final int r) {
  Ppl.drawCircle(x,y,r);}

 void drawHand
      (final int x, final int y, final double l, final int a) {
  double b = (a - 15) * 3.1415926 / 30;
  int x2 = x + (int) Math.round(l * Math.cos(b));
  int y2 = y + (int) Math.round(l * Math.sin(b));
  Ppl.drawLine(x,y,x2,y2);}

 void drawHourHand (final int x, final int y, final int r) {
  drawHand(x,y,r * 0.5,h * 5 + mn / 12);}

 void drawMinuteHand (final int x, final int y, final int r) {
  drawHand(x,y,r * 0.7,mn);}

 void draw (final int x, final int y, final int r) {
  drawDial(x,y,r);
  drawHourHand(x,y,r);
  drawMinuteHand(x,y,r);}}
```

An object of class `Clock` represents a point in time, for example {h = 13, mn = 58}. The method `draw` draws a clock of radius r centred at (x,y). This method uses others: `drawDial`, which draws a circle, `drawHand`, which draws a clock hand of length l and angle a measured from the vertical axis in sixtieths of a rotation, `drawHourHand`, and `drawMinuteHand`.

Now we would like to define another class called `ClockWithSeconds` such that an object of this class represents a point in time in terms of hours h, minutes mn and seconds s, for example {h = 14, mn = 2, s = 30}.

One way of doing this would be to define ClockWithSeconds as a completely independent type

```
class ClockWithSeconds {
  int h;
  int mn;
  int s;}
```

and another solution is to define a clock with seconds as a pair composed of a regular clock and an integer for the seconds

```
class ClockWithSeconds {
  Clock clock;
  int s;}
```

Java has a construct that allows the definition of a class as an extension of a class that is already defined by adding new fields and methods: *inheritance.*

We define the class ClockWithSeconds as an extension of the Clock class with the keyword extends

```
class ClockWithSeconds extends Clock {
  int s;

  ClockWithSeconds (final int x, final int y, final int z) {
    h = x; mn = y; s = z;}

  void drawSecondHand (final int x, final int y, final int r) {
    drawHand(x,y,r * 0.8,s);}

  void draw (final int x, final int y, final int r) {
    drawDial(x,y,r);
    drawHourHand(x,y,r);
    drawMinuteHand(x,y,r);
    drawSecondHand(x,y,r);}}
```

All the fields and methods of the class Clock are inherited in the new class.

It is also possible to redefine certain methods, like the method draw, which must be altered to draw the second hand.

All expressions of type ClockWithSeconds are also of type Clock. If h is an expression of type Clock created with the constructor Clock and k is an expression of type Clock created with the constructor ClockWithSeconds, the statements h.draw(40,40,30); and k.draw(40,40,30); draw a clock without a second hand in the first case, and with a second hand in the second.

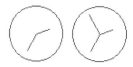

Inheritance allows you to give these two objects a different version of the `draw` method.

To conclude this short introduction of inheritance, which is a subject complex enough to occupy an entire book, we shall see how it can be applied to disjunctive types.

Exercise 8.5 (Disjunctive types)

Remember than an arithmetic expression is either a constant, a variable, the sum or two arithmetic expressions, or the product of two arithmetic expressions.

We define a type `Expr` with no fields or constructors, but with a method `print`, whose body is immaterial since it will never be executed.

```
class Expr {

  void print () {System.out.println("Hello");}}
```

1. Define four classes `Constant`, `Variable`, `Sum`, `Product` that extend the class `Expr`, respectively with a field of type `int`, a field of type `String`, two fields of type `Expr`, and two fields of type `Expr` and redefine the method `print`.

2. Define the value of type `Expr` corresponding to the expression `x + 3`. Print this expression.

3. Why can the statement `System.out.println("Hello");` never be executed?

4. What happens if you remove the class `Expr` and keep the four classes `Constant`, `Variable`, `Sum`, `Product`? What happens if you keep the class `Expr` but remove the method `print`?

5. Write a method that finds the derivative of an arithmetic expression with respect to a variable.

6. How would you add a new case, for example subtraction, to arithmetic expressions?

So there are essentially four ways to define disjunctive types in a programming language. The first is only possible when defining the disjunction of a cartesian product with a singleton — as in the case with lists. It consists of identifying the singleton element with the value null, if the language has such a value. The second is to use a selector field, which requires that the language allows the creation of a default value for each type. The third is to use a primitive construct for disjunctive types, if the language has one. The fourth uses inheritance, if the language allows for it.

8.7 Caml

Objects in Caml are somewhat different than in Java. In Java, records are special types of objects. In Caml, records and objects are completely different constructs. Another difference is that, in Caml, an object's fields can only be accessed by that object's methods. To allow other objects to access its fields, you must write a getter method, *such as* get_c *below. The last difference is that there are no static methods in Caml.*

As in Java, each field can be a constant or mutable, which is specified with the keyword mutable. *We create a new object with the keyword* new *and we access its methods using the symbol* #.

The class for a stack is defined, for example, as follows

```
class stack = object
 val mutable c = ([]:int list)
 method get_c () = c
 method testempty () = c = []
 method push x = c <- x::c
 method pop () = c <- List.tl c
 method top () = List.hd c
end
```

As Caml has no static methods, the function empty *that creates an empty stack cannot be a method of the class* stack *and is defined outside of the class*

```
let empty () = new stack
```

Then, we can use these methods and this function in a program

```
let p = empty () in
(p#push 5;
 p#push 6;
 print_int (p#top());
 print_newline();
 p#pop();
```

```
print_int (p#top());
print_newline ())
```

There are no objects in C. But there are objects in a language that is a successor to C, called C++.

9
Programming with Trees

9.1 Trees

We have seen that a tree type is a type in which several fields are recursive. When two fields are recursive, the type is called a *binary* tree type.

The simplest tree type is a binary tree type without any non-recursive fields.

```
class Tree {
 Tree left;
 Tree right;
}
```

A value of this type is either `null` or is a reference associated in memory with a record composed of two values of the same type.

G. Dowek, *Principles of Programming Languages*,
Undergraduate Topics in Computer Science, DOI 10.1007/978-1-84882-032-6_9,
© Springer-Verlag London Limited 2009

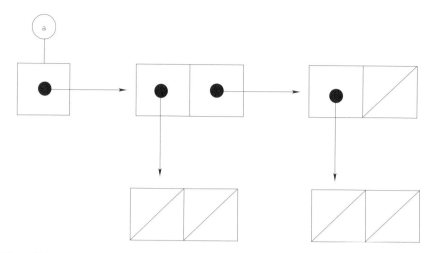

We will limit ourselves, in this chapter, to states in which the same reference is used only once. This will exclude infinite values

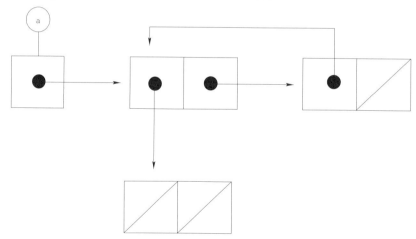

as well as those that will share a cell

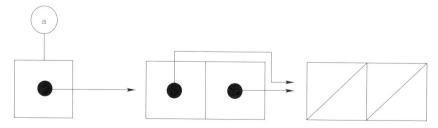

We will also use a more convenient notation for trees. Each cell will be represented by a circle. Instead of arrows, we will use line segments. The state represented in the first figure of this chapter can then be represented as

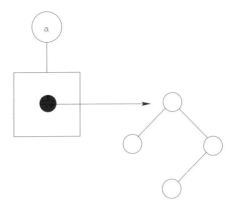

A *tree* is a value of type `Tree`, either the value `null` called the *empty tree* or a cell.

Let `r` be a tree that is a cell. The *nodes* of the tree `r` are the cells accessible from `r`, that is, the elements of the smallest set that contains `r` and that, if it contains a cell `c`, also contains the cell `c.left`, if this value is a cell and not the value `null`, and the cell `c.right`, if this value is a cell and not the value `null`. For example, the value of the variable `a` above is a tree that contains four nodes.

By convention, the set of nodes of the empty tree is the empty set.

The *size* of a tree is its number of nodes.

A node `d` is the *left child* of a node `c` if `d = c.left`, is the *right child* of a node `c` if `d = c.right`. The node `c` is the *parent* of the node `d` if `d` is a child of `c`. A node is a *leaf node* if it has no children. The cell `r`, seen as a node of the tree `r`, is called the *root* of the tree `r`. But, formally, a tree and its root are the same cell.

If `c` is a node of a tree `a`, then the trees `c.left` and `c.right` are called the left and right *sub-trees* of `c`. These trees can themselves be empty or not. Formally, the left child and the left sub-tree of a node, if it is not empty, are the same cell.

A *branch* of a tree is a sequence of nodes of `a` such that each element of the sequence is a child of the node that precedes it. The *height* of a tree `a` is the length of the longest branch of the tree, minus 1. For example, the length of the longest branch of the tree

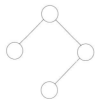

is 3 and the height of this tree is then 2. The height of a tree of a single node
is 0. By convention, the height of the empty tree is -1.

All of these definitions generalize immediately to trees with more fields,
recursive or not.

Exercise 9.1

Write a function that computes the number of leaves of a binary tree.
Write a function that computes the number of nodes of a binary tree.
Write a function that computes the number of internal nodes of a binary
tree.

A second tree type is obtained by adding, to the above type, a non recursive
field, for example of type int

```
class Tree {
 int val;
 Tree left;
 Tree right;}
```

In this case, the field val of a node c is called the *contents* of node c.

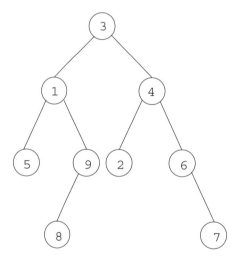

9.2 Traversing a Tree

The traversal of a tree is an operation consisting of applying an operation p to
each node of a tree, typically printing the contents of the node. We then say
that we have *visited* each of the nodes of the tree.

As we are applying the same operation p to each node, two traversals of the same tree can only differ by the order in which the nodes are visited. The traversal of a tree can then also be defined as an order over the nodes of this tree.

Two common types of traversal are the *depth first* and the *breadth first*.

9.2.1 Depth First Traversal

When using depth first traversal, you start at the root, descend the length of the leftmost branch until arriving at a leaf, then climb this branch, descending as soon as possible down another branch.

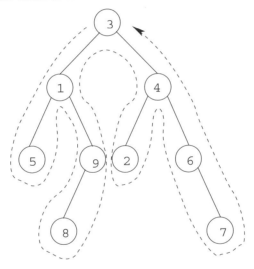

There are several different types of depth first tree traversal. If you visit a node before descending its left sub-tree, it is known as a *preorder* traversal. If you visit a node after returning from the left sub-tree but before descending the right sub-tree, it is known as an *inorder* traversal. If you visit a node after visiting both the left and right sub-trees, it is known as *postorder*.

In the above example, a preorder traversal visits the nodes in the order 3 1 5 9 8 4 2 6 7, an inorder traversal visits the nodes in the order 5 1 8 9 3 2 4 6 7, and a postorder traversal visits the nodes in the order 5 8 9 1 2 7 6 4 3.

A depth first traversal can be programmed using a while loop and a list that contains the sub-trees waiting to be traversed. We start by adding a single element to the list: the tree a. Then, as long as the list is not empty, we examine its first element. If this tree is empty, we remove it from the list. If it is a singleton tree, we visit its only node. Otherwise, we decompose the tree into three smaller trees: its left sub-tree, its right sub-tree, and the singleton tree formed by its root, and we add these three trees to the list. Since these three trees must be traversed before the rest in the list, this list should be a stack.

When performing an inorder traversal, we traverse these three trees in the order: left, root, right, and can be added to the stack in reverse order.

```
Stack p = Stack.empty ();
p.push(a);
 while (!(p.testempty())) {
  Tree b = p.top ();
  p.pop();
  if (b != null) {
   if (singleton(b))
    System.out.print(b.val + " ");
    else {
     p.push(b.right);
     p.push(new Tree(b.val,null,null));
     p.push(b.left);}}}
```

By changing the order in which you add the three sub-trees to the stack, you can program a preorder or postorder traversal.

You can avoid using a stack by programming the traversal recursively

```
static void traverse (Tree a) {
 if (a != null) {
  traverse(a.left);
  System.out.print(a.val + " ");
  traverse(a.right);}}
```

Exercise 9.2

Write a function that performs a preorder traversal and one that performs a postorder traversal.

Exercise 9.3

What is outputted during a preorder, inorder, and postorder traversal of the following tree?

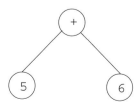

And for the following trees?

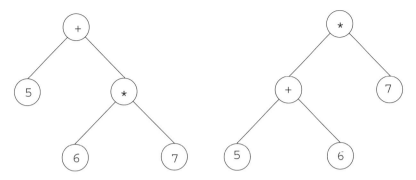

9.2.2 Breadth First Traversal

A breadth first traversal consists of visiting the root, then all of the children of the root, from left to right, then all of the grandchildren of the root, ...

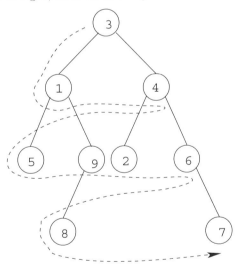

This can be programmed like the depth first traversal using a `while` loop and a list of sub-trees waiting to be traversed. When you remove an element from the list, you visit its root and add its left and right sub-trees to the list. Unlike depth first traversal, these sub-trees can only be visited after visiting all of the trees already in the list. The stack is therefore replaced with a queue.

```
Queue p = Queue.empty ();
p.add(a);
while (!(p.testempty())) {
```

```
Tree b = p.fst ();
p.suppress();
if (b != null) {
 System.out.print(b.val + " ");
 p.add(b.left);
 p.add(b.right);}}
```

In the above example, a breadth first traversal visits the nodes in the order 3 1 4 5 9 2 6 8 7.

You can also eliminate the `while` loop by using recursion, but unlike recursive depth first traversal, you still require the use of a queue.

9.3 Search Trees

9.3.1 Membership

In Chapter 6, we have seen that a finite set can be represented with a list and that with this representation, testing to see if an element belongs to this set or not requires a linear average time with respect to the number of elements in the set.

Now imagine we wanted to find a word in the dictionary by searching through each and every entry, from cover to cover. We already know a more efficient method for looking up words in the dictionary: you open the dictionary roughly in the middle, compare your word with the median entry, which eliminates half of the dictionary. Recursively apply the same procedure to remaining half, and you will eventually find your word.

This method of *binary search* requires logarithmic time with respect to the size of the dictionary. However, this method depends on the fact that the dictionary is ordered by word, and that words can be accessed randomly with constant time, which is the case with a book, but would not be true for a papyrus scroll.

Representing a set by a list does not allow for a binary search, because even if the list is ordered, accessing the median element of the list requires linear time, and not constant time, with respect to the size of the list.

In contrast, a binary search is possible if you replace the list with an array. But this solution has two problems. The size of an array must be known in advance, and it is not possible to change its size after it has been created. Also, adding a new element to an array requires linear time with respect to the size of the array, since it becomes necessary to shift all of the elements larger than the one being inserted.

The solution to allow for searching, inserting, and removing an element in logarithmic time is to use a search tree. A *search tree* is a binary tree where each node contains an element, and all of the elements appearing in the left sub-tree of a node are smaller than the element contained in this node, and all of the elements appearing in the right sub-tree of a node are larger than the element contained in this node. A set can be represented by a search tree in different ways. For example, the set {1, 5, 9, 12, 19, 24} can be represented by the search trees

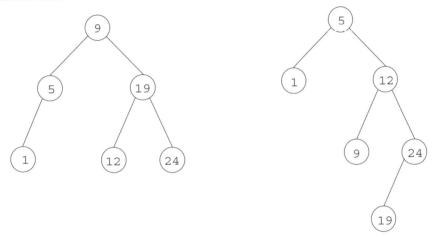

To test for the membership of an element with a set represented by a search tree, we start by testing to see if the tree is empty. If this is the case, we return the boolean `false`. If not, we compare the element to be found with the element contained in the root of the tree. If these two elements are the same, we return the value `true`. If the element to be found is smaller than the element contained in the root, then we can ignore the right sub-tree and recursively apply the same algorithm to the left sub-tree. If the element to be found is larger than the element contained in the root, we ignore the left sub-tree and recursively apply the algorithm to the right sub-tree. The time required to see if an element is contained in the set or not is, in the worst case, linear in the height of the tree.

To program this search in Java, we can choose to use a static method, which allows us to use the function even when the tree is empty.

```
static boolean search (final int x, final Tree a) {
  if (a == null) return false;
  if (x == a.val) return true;
  if (x < a.val) return search (x,a.left);
  return search (x,a.right);}
```

Similarly, inserting a new element in the tree requires a time linear in the height of the tree. We choose a method that modifies its argument and not a method that copies it. This method returns a tree that is the result of this insertion. Note that when you execute `insert(a);`, the value of `a` after the method has been executed is the result of this insertion, except in the case where `a` is the empty tree.

```
static Tree insert (final int x, final Tree a) {
  if (a == null) return new Tree(x,null,null);
  if (x < a.val) {a.left = insert(x,a.left); return a;}
  if (x > a.val) {a.right = insert(x,a.right); return a;}
  return a;}
```

The removal of an element of a tree also requires a time linear in the height of the tree, but the method of doing so is somewhat more difficult than searching and insertion. Once the node to remove has been found, there are three possible cases. If this node is a leaf, it can simply be removed. If this node has only one child, it can be deleted, and its child connected directly to its parent. If this node has two children, then you must find the largest element of its left sub-tree, replace the removed node by this element and then recursively remove this element from the left sub-tree.

Note that the removal of these elements in the left sub-tree can be done in a single step, since the largest element in a tree cannot have a right child.

```
static int max (final Tree a) {
  if (a.right == null) return a.val; else return (max(a.right));}
```

```
static Tree remove (final int x, final Tree a) {
  if (a == null) return null;
  if (x == a.val) {
    if ((a.left == null) && (a.right == null)) return null;
    else if (a.left == null) return a.right;
    else if (a.right == null) return a.left;
    else {int m = max(a.left);
          a.val = m;
          a.left = remove(m,a.left);
          return a;}}
  if (x < a.val) {a.left = remove(x,a.left);return a;}
  a.right = remove(x,a.right);return a;}
```

Exercise 9.4

In order to program these functions using dynamic methods, and that these methods can modify their argument including when the tree is empty, a solution is to create a wrapper type for these trees.

Rewrite these three methods for this wrapper class for trees.

9.3.2 Balanced Trees

In a binary tree, the root has at most 2^1 children, 2^2 grandchildren, 2^3 great grandchildren, ... The maximum size of a binary tree of height h is then $2^0 + 2^1 + 2^2 + \ldots + 2^h = 2^{h+1} - 1$. Because of this, when a number n is such that $2^{h+1} \leq n < 2^{h+2}$, it is possible to construct a binary tree of size n of height $h + 1$, but not one of height h. The minimum height of a tree of size n is thus $\lfloor \log_2(n) \rfloor$, the floor of the binary logarithm of n. A tree is said to be of *minimal height* if its height is equal to $\lfloor \log_2(n) \rfloor$ where n is its size. The complexity of searching, insertion, and removal of an element in a tree of minimal height is thus logarithmic with respect to the size of the tree.

However, the maximal height of a tree of size n is $n - 1$.

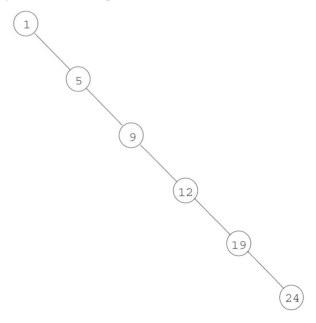

The complexity of searching, insertion, and removal of an element in a tree of maximal height is thus linear — and not logarithmic — with respect to the size of the tree.

The height of a tree of size n is therefore between $\lfloor \log_2(n) \rfloor$ and $n - 1$. We can show that if we construct a tree by inserting n distinct elements in random order, then the expected value of the height of the tree is linear in $\ln(n)$. The expected value of the time required to search, insert or remove an element is thus logarithmic. But, this is only the expected value for complexity, and worse cases may emerge. In particular, if you insert, which is unfortunately often the case, elements that are already ordered into a search tree, you obtain a tree of maximal height.

To ensure that searching, insertion and removal in a tree occur in logarithmic time with respect to the size of the tree in all cases, you must ensure that the tree remains balanced when you insert or remove an element. A natural solution would be to require that the trees remain of minimal height. But due to the re-balancing cost, it then seems to be impossible to find insertion and removal algorithms that occur in logarithmic time, although the non-existence of such algorithms seems to be only a conjecture. We can, however, impose less strict conditions that allow for a logarithmic complexity for searching, insertion, and removal.

A set of trees is called a *set of balanced trees*, if there exists a number k such that all the non-empty trees of n nodes belonging to this set have a height less than k ln(n). The set of trees of minimal height, for example, is a set of balanced trees, but not the set of all trees.

Note that every finite set of trees is a set of balanced trees. Because of this, all trees appear in at least one set of balanced trees. It is therefore important, when we say a tree is balanced, to specify the set to which we are referring.

Also note that it is equivalent to require that there exist a number k and a number N such that all trees of n nodes have a height less than k ln(n), for all n ≥ N.

One method to render searching, insertion, and removal of a node logarithmic in all cases is to choose a set of balanced trees and to use algorithms for insertion and removal that keep the tree in this set. Many examples of balanced trees for which such algorithms exist have been proposed: Adel'son-Velskii and Landis trees, 2-3 trees, bi-coloured trees, ...

For example, a tree is an *Adel'son-Velskii and Landis tree*, or AVL, if the difference in height of the left and right sub-trees of each node is always equal to 0 or to 1. We can show that the height of such a tree is bounded from above by ln(n + 2) / ln(τ) - 1 where τ = (1 + $\sqrt{5}$) / 2 and thus, when n is larger than 4, the height of such a tree is bounded from above by ln(n) / ln(τ). Thus, AVL trees form a set of balanced trees.

When we apply the standard methods of insertion and removal to an AVL tree, we obtain a tree that is not necessarily AVL. All of the nodes of a branch of the tree can become unbalanced. We must then re-balance each of these nodes, by employing *rotations*. A *right rotation* is the following transformation

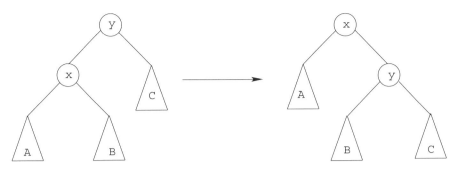

and a *left rotation* is the inverse of a right rotation. Such rotations transform
a search tree into another search tree.

Exercise 9.5

We consider a tree such that the two sub-trees of a root are AVL but
such that the difference of the height of these two sub-trees are equal to
2.

Show that you can transform this tree into an AVL tree by applying
rotations to the root and its children.

We distinguish several cases based on the height of the trees whose roots
are the children and grandchildren of the root of the tree to balance.

Exercise 9.6

Write in Java functions for insertion and removal of elements from AVL
trees. How can you avoid having to compute the height of a tree — which
requires a linear time and not a logarithmic time with respect to its size?

9.3.3 Dictionaries

In Chapter 6, we have seen that an association list is a representation of a
function with a finite domain, typically a dictionary, of the form of a list of
pairs such that for all k, there exists at most an element v such that the pair
(k,v) belongs to the list.

Searching for a value associated with a key in an association list is linear
with respect to the number of pairs. By replacing the list with a search tree,
ordered on its keys, we can do search, insertion, and removal in logarithmic
time.

Exercise 9.7

Define in Java a type of tree for dictionaries. Write methods for searching,
insertion, and removal for these trees.

9.4 Priority Queues

9.4.1 Partially Ordered Trees

Remember that a priority queue is a set in which each element is given a priority. Operations on such a set are searching for the element with the highest priority, insertion of an element, and removal of an element with the highest priority. In Chapter 6, we have seen that we can represent a priority queue with a list, but that searching for an element and removing an element with the highest priority occurs in linear time, unless we decide to order the elements of this list by priority, in which case insertion becomes linear.

We can render searching, insertion, and removal of an element from a priority list logarithmic by using a tree, for example a balanced search tree. However, there is a simpler solution. A binary tree is said to be *partially ordered* if the contents of a child of a node are always smaller than the contents of this node. For example, the set {1, 5, 9, 12, 19, 24} can be represented by the following partially ordered trees

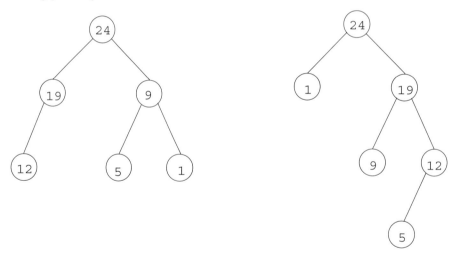

Searching for the maximum element in a partially ordered tree is easy, since this element must be the contents of the root of the tree. The time required to find it is independent of the size of the tree.

Removal of the maximum element is not difficult either, and illustrates the mechanism of promotion in a hierarchical structure: the boss dies, the best deputy of the boss becomes boss, the best deputy of the deputy becomes deputy, ... The time required to remove an element is linear in the height of the tree.

Insertion is done in a similar fashion, by adding the new element anywhere it will fit, and to permute it with its parent if it is larger, and with its new parent, ... The time required to insert an element is linear in the height of the tree.

9.4.2 Partially Ordered Balanced Trees

Once again, to ensure that the operations of insertion and removal are logarithmic, you must balance the tree. Here, in contrast to the case of search trees, it is possible to ensure that the tree is always of minimum size, and even that it is *packed*, that is to say that the nodes of the bottom level are all located as far left as possible. For example, the first of the trees below is packed, but not the second, although both are of minimum height.

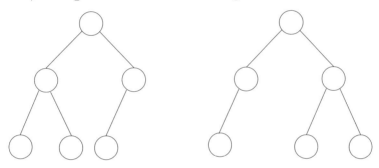

To precisely define the concept of a packed tree, we can introduce a numbering of the nodes of a tree. If `a` is a tree, we designate the node of a tree with an expression of the form `a.left.right.left.left`. The sequence of the fields `left right left left` can be read as a binary number by replacing `left` with `0` and `right` with `1` by adding a `1` to the start of the sequence to prevent it from starting with a `0`. Thus, we associate a different integer to each node of a tree: we associate the number `1` to the root and the numbers `2 n` and `2 n + 1` to the left and right children of a node associated with the number `n`. And a tree is *packed* if the numbers of its nodes form an interval of the form `1 ... n`.

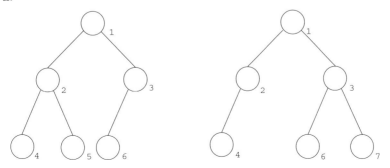

A packed, partially ordered tree is called a *heap*. This notion of a heap has nothing to do with the notion of a set of cells, as seen before.

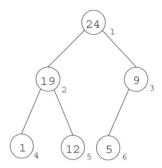

Like all partially ordered trees, we can find the maximum element in a heap in a time independent of the size of the heap, since the maximum element is contained in the root.

Adding an element occurs in logarithmic time. We start by adding the new element in the first empty space that keeps the tree packed, and we permute this element with its parent while it is larger than its parent, which reorders the tree.

To remove the maximum element, we replace the root by the element with the largest number — the lowest right element in the tree — so that the tree remains packed, and we permute it with the largest of its children while it is smaller than one of its children.

Exercise 9.8

Write in Java functions for searching, insertion, and removal of an element in a heap.

Since the numbers of a packed tree are contiguous, we can represent such a tree with an array by putting the contents of the node with number `i + 1` in compartment `i` of the array. The children of the node of compartment `i` — node of number `i + 1` — are in compartments `2 i + 1` and `2 i + 2` and the parent of the node of compartment `i` is in compartment `(i - 1) / 2`.

If compartments `0 ... i - 1` of an array represent a heap, the insertion in the heap of the element located in compartment `i` of the array is written as follows

```
static void insert (final int [] t, final int i) {
 int j = i;
 while (j >= 1 && t[(j-1)/2] <= t[j]) {
 int z = t[j]; t[j] = t[(j-1)/2];t[(j-1)/2] = z;j = (j-1)/2;}}
```

And if compartments 0 ... i of an array represent a heap, the removal from
the heap of the element located in compartment 0 of the array is written as
follows

```
static void remove (final int [] t, final int i) {
 t[0] = t[i];
 int j = 0;
 while ((2*j+1 < i && t[j] <= t[2*j+1])
        || (2*j+2 < i && t[j] <= t[2*j+2])) {
  int m = 2*j+1;
  if (m + 1 < i && t[m + 1] >= t[m]) m = m + 1;
  int z = t[j]; t[j] = t[m];t[m] = z;
  j = m;}}
```

Exercise 9.9

We can also represent priority queues with an AVL tree. Program methods for finding the element with the highest priority, insertion, and removal of the element with the highest priority using an AVL tree, in
logarithmic time.

Exercise 9.10 (Image Compression)

The simplest method of representing an image is in the form of an array
of numbers, each number being the colour of a pixel. Thus, a black and
white image of 256 pixels by 256 pixels can be represented with an **array**
of 65536 numbers whose values are either 0 or 1.

However, with an image such as

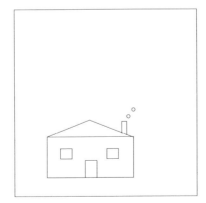

whose first 128 lines are white, the array would start with 32768 zeros.

A more efficient alternative, is to use a quaternary tree. We represent a
monochrome image by a singleton tree whose single node contains the

colour of the image. When an image is not monochrome, we divide it in four

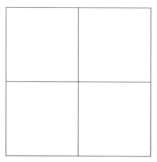

We compute the tree of each of its four sub-images and we construct a quaternary tree composed of a root with no content and these four sub-trees. Thus, the tree of the above image has the form

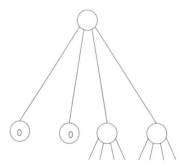

and expressing that the top half of the image is entirely white requires only two nodes of the tree.

Write a function that transforms an array of 0 and 1 into a tree and vice-versa.

Index

allocation, 61
argument
– formal, 21
– real, 21
argument passing
– by reference (or by variable), 39
– by value, 39
array, 79
assignment, 1

binary search, 146
`boolean`, 3
branch of a tree, 141
`byte`, 3

`catch`, 122
cell, 61
– free, 98
`char`, 3
child
– left, 141
– right, 141
class, 60
– static, 133
`class`, 26, 60
complexity, 113
– average, 113
– worst case, 113
computable, 17
concatenation, 105
`const`, 5
`constant`, 5
constructor, 64, 93
contents of a node of a tree, 142

core
– functional, 55
– imperative, 1

definition
– function, 20
– recursive, 48
`do`, 16
`double`, 3
dynamic data, 85

environment, 9
– global, 29
equality
– physical, 68
– structural, 68
error message, 124
`Exception`, 122
exception, 122
`exception`, 125
expression, 1
– arithmetical, 90
`extends`, 135

`false`, 3
fifo, 118
`float`, 3
`for`, 16
function, 20
function body, 20
function call, 20

garbage collection, 98
`giveup`, 14

157

Printed in the United States